MW01592058

Living in Destruction

by Gloria Leigh Wilhite

RoseDog🐾Books

PITTSBURGH, PENNSYLVANIA 15238

The contents of this work including, but not limited to, the accuracy of events, people, and places depicted; opinions expressed; permission to use previously published materials included; and any advice given or actions advocated are solely the responsibility of the author, who assumes all liability for said work and indemnifies the publisher against any claims stemming from publication of the work.

All Rights Reserved
Copyright © 2018 by Gloria Leigh Wilhite

No part of this book may be reproduced or transmitted, downloaded, distributed, reverse engineered, or stored in or introduced into any information storage and retrieval system, in any form or by any means, including photocopying and recording, whether electronic or mechanical, now known or hereinafter invented without permission in writing from the publisher.

RoseDog Books
585 Alpha Drive, Suite 103
Pittsburgh, PA 15238
Visit our website at www.rosedogbookstore.com

ISBN: 978-1-4809-8127-0
eISBN: 978-1-4809-8104-1

Foreword

I'd like to thank God, our Father,
for being in my life and guiding me.

Best wishes to my good friends who encouraged me to keep writing:
Haines Sigurdsson and his son Duncan Sigurdsson,
Mrs. Marilyn Mattson,
and Jerry Boutin.

My thanks and prayers to all of you.

The Florida sun came up bright and hot as usual for a day in late August. A very tired mother was in labor and getting nowhere. Dr. B came in to check her over. Her last child had been born by C-section and so this one would be as well.

She worried about Dr. B. It was rumored that since he came back from serving as a surgeon in the Korean War, he was an alcoholic and gave himself shots of morphine in an attempt to deaden the memories of what he saw and experienced there. But what was she to do? He was the only doctor for several counties around central Florida, and he owned the only hospital. It was the Theresa Holland Hospital.

The mother's name was Mildred. She was 36 years old, white, very poor, and had three more children at home. She truly hoped this would be the last one.

Dr. B said he'd be back after rounds to deliver the baby. No one knows the exact time of her birth, but the doctor did rounds early in the morning, and it was assumed the baby girl was born about 8:30 a.m. Mama began to hemorrhage due to a rupture of the placenta. She went into a coma. I was born and weighed only five pounds, one ounce, and was placed in an incubator, where I lived for the next three months. No one has ever been able to tell me why. I have always been told that my mother and I came very close to death. Mama used to tell me that the only reason we survived was by "the grace of God."

And so, I was named Gloria.

My grandmother came and stayed at Mama's side, praying for her and reading to her from the Bible. Mama said she came so close to dying that she saw "the Pearly Gates of Heaven." When she came out of her coma, her mother was still reading the Bible to her.

This was 1951. They didn't know all that they know now. I went home three months later, and Mama and I didn't get to know each other or get to form a bond until I went home. You have to remember she had a husband and three children at home. My oldest brother, Gene, was fifteen years old, then Eddie was eight years old, and my sister Loretta was five-and-a-half years old. Mama still had to heal from the C-section and the loss of blood. She was in a lot of pain and very weak. I am not sure who came to help, but it was most likely my grandmother or my Aunt Etta, my mother's sister.

I don't know if we had a car at the time or not; we usually didn't. There was no money for taxis, and we lived on the outskirts of town. Mama was trying to heal; she couldn't walk all the way to town to see me, hold me, cuddle me, or whisper sweet words of love that a child needs to hear.

When I came home, my baby bed was a large dresser drawer that was lined with thick blankets. We had a mama cat that slept with me in Mama and Daddy's bedroom. Mama's milk had dried up, and I couldn't keep cow's milk down. An elderly neighbor lady down the road came up and brought her nanny goat to Mama.

"I understand you have a new baby that doesn't like cow milk," she told Mama. "I will teach you how to care for the goat and how to milk her."

I was raised on goat milk and did very well.

When I was about a year old, we moved across town to live beside Green Swamp in Leesburg, Florida. We were extremely poor. I probably did not realize this until I was nearly grown. We were blessed though because my father had grown up on a farm. We always had a garden in our back yard. Sometimes dinner was five vegetables. If we were lucky and someone went fishing or hunting, then we would have meat. On Sundays, Daddy always made sure we had fried chicken. Sometimes, if the markets were down on hogs or cattle, then my uncles would come over and get my brothers and go gator hunting. It was not illegal at the time. They would gut the gators and give the tail meat to the families and sell the hides to designers in New York City. Pretty smart, huh?

Now, Mama could bake almost anything. She made wonderful iced tea and crispy fried chicken, but give her a roast beef, and she would cook it until it was like leather. If it was turtle, fish, squirrel, or rabbit, she could cook it and make it taste wonderful. Mama was also a talented seamstress. She could take my sister to a dress store and have her try on the latest styles. If my sister liked a dress, my mama would turn the dress inside out and study the seams to see how to make it. They would buy the fabric and such on their way home, and Mama would cut out the fabric without a pattern. One time, someone gave her an old coat that you'd think was no good. She took it apart, turned it inside out to the silk lining and made me a winter coat like the child star Shirley Temple wore. I was so proud of it! That was the first coat that I remember. We didn't always have coats. My Aunt Etta used to always make sure that I had a new one each school year.

We lived in the deep south—can't get much deeper when you live right next to a swamp! Daddy used to hire an old black man to work for him. Daddy was a master carpenter. He would bring the old man home with him for dinner at noon. I never knew his name. Mr... Somebody. I was about four or five and wasn't in school at the time, and it was my job to get his meal for him. Daddy always invited him into the house to the table. The old man always declined. He always said there could be trouble if anyone in town found out he was working with a black man.

Daddy told him, "Do not worry about it."

As far as I know, there was never any trouble. The old man would find a shady oak tree and sit beneath it. I would go in to Mama, and she would give me a plate full of beans, greens, and cornbread for him. Along with it came a large mayonnaise jar full of iced tea. When he finished, I would take his dishes inside and refill them. He always ate all of it, and I used to ask Mama if he was a poor man.

Mama said, "Honey, he is poorer than we are."

When dinner was finished, the old man would lean back under the oak tree and take a nap. I would take his dishes inside to Mama. Back then, the men who worked outdoors would take off from noon to 2 or 3 p.m. That way they got out of the sun and rested, then went back and worked until dark. I would climb up on Mama's stomach and lay down with her and Daddy, and we'd all take a nap. I can still remember how soft Mama's stomach was and warm. I could hear her regular, strong heart beat that would lull me to sleep. It always made me feel loved, and I would calm down and finally fall asleep.

My oldest brother, Gene, had Mama sign for him at sixteen years of age to join the Marine Corps. This was during the Korean War. I was only a year old. He made it a career of 23-and-a-half years. Because of his combat experience, they wanted him to stay in the Corps when his retirement date came up. He was a Staff Sergeant, and they offered him a chance to become a Captain. He turned them down. He and I got to know each other after I was grown. He once wrote a letter, when he was serving in Vietnam telling us that they had to get their water from the local river. Then, they had to add chlorine tablets to the water so they could drink it. That was horrible!

I began sending him pre-sweetened Kool-Aid for them to add to the water to improve the taste. I used my own babysitting money to pay for it. He wrote that when he got one of my care packages, the guys would gather around for a package of Kool-Aid. He is now my brother and friend of many years. He still works out on a fitness ma-

4

chine, two hours a day. He looks great but is getting old. He lives in New Mexico with his wife.

The other thing that happened when I was a year old was that my other brother, who was eight years old, got into trouble and was sent away to the Dozier School for Boys in Marianna, Florida. He came home at some point and then was sent away again when he was 10 years old.

We seldom had a car. But one year at Easter, we were blessed with one, so we went up to see Eddie. Mama made a baked ham, sweet potatoes, potato salad, coleslaw, and pie. They had picnic tables where we could set up and visit. While Mama and Daddy fixed dinner, Eddie and I sat and visited. I was about four or five years old, and Eddie was about twelve. He came home the next year. There was a small white house nearby.

I asked Eddie, "Who lives there?"

He said, "No one. That's the White House."

"What's that?" I asked.

"When you break the rules, or if they think you've been bad, they take you in there and make you take off your clothes and make you climb up on the gurney," he said. "Then they strap you down with leather. Sometimes, they touch you like they are not supposed to. That's awful, and you can't do anything about it. Then they take leather belts and beat us until blood hits the walls and the floor. Some kids got beat enough that the blood hits the ceiling."

Then he told me that some black kids didn't make it. He saw a couple of black boys taken out dead.

He did not get to come home until he was 13 years old. The school closed down around the 1980s or the 1990s. In a later investigation, authorities found three previously unknown cemeteries of unknown children that had died there and simply had a white cross on their spot. Only one out of all of those children was identified in the bones that were found and was sent to his family. I could go on, but this book is about me, not my brothers.

When Ed was home, he was my playmate. When I was five years, old he came home from the school. He taught me how to shoot a 22cal. rifle with his help. He also taught me how to balance a knife, and I learned to throw it by the handle or by the blade. Then he taught me how to "Indian Fight." I did fairly well for a skinny, little five-year-old girl. We have a very special mental connection.

After Ed came home, he and Mama didn't get along too well. One Sunday, we were having dinner, and everyone was quiet. We were all enjoying the meal.

Mama asked Ed, "Do you like your dinner?"

He answered, "Yes."

Then Mama said, "No, you don't! You're just saying that."

Ed said, "Yes, mama, I do like dinner. It's the best fried chicken that I have had in a long time."

Mama took off her shoe, threw it at Ed, and caught him in the face with it. Mostly what I remember is a lot of yelling and screaming. Then, all of a sudden, the police were there. They said Ed had to go with them. I didn't like that. I was five years old, and they were going to take my Bubba, and I wasn't having any of it. As they were trying to put handcuffs on him, I kicked that cop in the shin. When he didn't let go of my brother, I sank my sharp little teeth into the cop's leg. Ed had to explain to me that he had to go with them because he "had been a bad boy."

I said, "No! You're not a bad boy, but Mama was bad and hit you for no reason."

That didn't seem to matter because he had to leave, and I never saw him again until he was 18 years old and married. My cousin David told me that some people in Coleman, named the Robinsons or the Robertsons, took him in at fifteen years old. I never knew that until I was in my 50s. They have already passed on, and their home just sits, falling apart.

I was born with what was called "lazy eye," or amblyopia. The doctor tried having me wear a black eye patch on my left eye to try to make the right eye work. Poor Mama became a nervous wreck and finally took it off. I was to have eye surgery. On the day that we were being picked up by my Aunt Lilly Schoblum, our bathroom had a wood fueled hot water heater, and when I got out of the bath, I bumped my bare bottom against the heater and burned my little butt. I cried and cried.

Daddy came home for dinner, and he gave me some gum to try to make me feel better. I cried and cried, then Aunt Lilly got there. I had to sit on a pillow all the way to Ocala. That's where I had to go to have surgery. Mama was with me. At five-and-a-half years old, I had to have surgery on my right eye. Right after my surgery, I woke up and could not see. No one had warned me of this. Both eyes were bandaged and I was very afraid and began crying out for my mother. Mama heard me from the waiting room and came running into recovery.

A nurse tried to stop mama, and she said, "That's my baby in there, and you better move!"

The nurse didn't move, so Mama knocked her down and came to me!

I shared a room with another little girl who cried all the time. Our mothers took turns reading to us or telling us stories to try to keep our minds off of what was going on.

One day, I noticed the little girl was not crying. I could not see her because I still had patches on my eyes. I asked Mama why the little girl wasn't crying.

"She died," Mama said, and added, "she had a disease called Muscular Dystrophy, and it is very painful."

That was my first encounter with death. I have often wondered if they had pain medicine for children or not. It was 1956, and many new things were being invented. I never knew her name. But, I'll never forget her.

One year, my sister and I both became ill with the measles and ear infections. One night, I was crying so much from pain that Mama took me outside on the porch and rocked me in her old weather-beaten rocking chair. She had a beautiful Irish voice and would sing to me. I felt so warm and loved when she did that. She could surprise you. At least that was a good surprise. I loved that old rocking chair.

During this time period, Daddy had a car. It was summertime, so Daddy would drop us off at the lake to swim. We stayed there until he picked us up. One morning, we got there and heard a mama cat crying. There were two dead kittens in the trash can. There were a couple more kittens roaming around on the beach. One was getting into the water, and I ran and picked it up. Their eyes were not open yet. Then we looked around and found the mama cat. A gator had ripped her open, and she tried to hide between some rocks. Her intestines were hanging out of her body. We very carefully put her and her kittens together on our blanket. We dripped water into their mouths as best we could. When Daddy came to get us, we had the mother and kittens in our blanket, and with the faith of children, we took them home for Mama to heal them. Daddy always wanted his dinner when he got home from work. Well, not that day. Mama gave kittens to me and my sister with some warmed milk and droppers to feed them.

"They must be fed every two hours," she explained. "That is your job."

She gave us all rigid instructions to stay out of her kitchen and be very quiet. She had an enamel table where she prepared our food. She cleaned it with bleach and a scrub brush. After being thoroughly bleached and rinsed again with boiling water she let it air dry and then placed soft, clean towels on the table. She placed the mama cat on the towels. The poor mama cat made a low growl due to the pain. Mama took down a pint of whiskey that was used for medicinal purposes. She poured some whiskey into a teaspoon and poured it down the mama cat's throat to try to help with the pain. She didn't know what else to do. During this time, water had been on boil with a little salt. Once it was boiling mama added sewing needles and thick, white sewing thread to the pot. Then, it was set aside to cool.

Mama spoke softly to the cat to try to keep her calm. Mama told the kitty everything she was doing and that she would try to help her. Mama kept speaking to her softly and quietly singing to her. Mama went to the sink and scrubbed and scrubbed her hands so they were very clean. She then gave mama cat another dose of whiskey and then gently brought her intestines out and rinsed them thoroughly with the cooled, salted water to get the dirt, grass, and twigs off of them.

Then, she gently placed them back into the mama cat and told us, "This Kitty was lucky. The gator did not manage to puncture anything."

Mama talked to the kitty and explained what she was doing next. Mama gave her another spoonful of whiskey. Then, Mama began to stitch the cat's abdomen. She used the sterilized needles and thread. The poor mama cat very quietly growled while Mama sewed her up. Mama continued to talk to her and prayed to God to help her know what to do. When she finished the stitching, she gave the cat more whiskey and gave her a few minutes to settle down. Then she sprinkled on sulfa powder and bandaged her with old, white strips of linen. Then, Mama mashed up some of our dinner and fed little bits to her. She gave her sips of water and finished it off with another spoonful of whiskey. We made a bed for her in a box and made another bed for her kittens and placed it beside the mama cat. We put the kittens into this second box. We continued the care, and the kittens grew up to be strong and healthy. We gave them new homes. The mama cat healed fine, but she never had more kittens. Her eyes twinkled like stars so we named her Twinkles. She began riding around on my shoulder.

One day, Mama was angry with me and pulled back her hand to slap me. All hell broke loose. Twinkles launched herself at Mama's face with her nails out. The cat and I ran off until Daddy got home. Mama gave him the whole story.

Daddy said, "Well, I guess we have to get rid of her."

Then, Mama said, "I don't think so. With all the snakes and such around here, I'd rather her stay and keep Gloria safe."

And so, it was decided that she stay with us, and she did until she died.

All I know is that some man took some sort of pictures of my sister. I can't help but wonder if it was child pornography. Mama made the man pay some money to keep her from calling the cops on him. Then, my sister went to live at our grandmother's house, which was 15 miles away. I don't remember seeing her again until she was 16 years old. She was 11 years old when this came about. Sometimes we had a car, and sometimes we didn't. I don't remember going to Grandma's during any of that time. They were only 15 miles from us. I thought my Aunt Etta would bring her to see us, but she didn't.

When Loretta came home, she got a job with WT Grant. It was a general merchandise store. She had her own apartment downtown. She met her husband Earl while working there, then married him and moved away to Staten Island in New York City. About a year and a half later, she gave birth to her first child. I can't really say that I missed her. All I had known was pain and abuse at her hands. That was how she treated her own children, and they came to hate her for it. She was always beating on them with her fists. I once asked her if the bad man that took her pictures had "touched her in a bad way." She said she couldn't remember but thought it might have happened. She has now left this Earth and is hopefully at peace.

I did not miss my sister very much. One day, she was up in one of the oak trees with some rocks. She told me to shut up, or she was going to drop a rock on my head. Evidently, I was quite a talker when I was little. Sure enough, I didn't shut up, and she dropped a rock on me, cutting me just above my left eye, which was my good eye. Mama kept trying to get her to come down out of the tree and she wouldn't. Daddy got home from work and heard the tale. He assessed me and got really angry. She was always doing things to hurt me. Daddy, I'm told, had to climb up the tree about 10 p.m. to drag her out of it. I heard she got quite a licking for that one.

At other times, such as when Mama and Daddy went grocery shopping, they would leave her to watch me. She would get one of Daddy's belts and beat the fire out of me. They would come home and I would have angry, red welts all over me. She'd get it again but always continued to do it. She was just pure mean.

I don't remember much else until about 10 years old, except for my seventh birthday. Mama cooked turtle soup on an outside fire, and I think most of the neighborhood came over. My friend, Brenda, gave me a well-used Barbie doll for my birthday. It had no clothes, and almost no hair. She and her sister, Linda, shared the doll but wanted me to have it. That was my only birthday gift. I don't even remember a cake. When I was eight years old, we moved to a better neighborhood across town. I liked it but not my new teachers so much. This is when Mama began to get sick.

We would walk downtown, and Mama would give me a quarter for the movies. It was 15 cents to get in, and 10 cents for a bag of lemon drops. Then she would go off to the bar. When the double feature was over, I would ask the counter lady to call the Magnolia for me. They would get Mama on the line for me, and she would bring me more money. I don't know where Daddy was. Probably working. You have no idea how I felt to see my mother walking wobbly from the bar down the street towards me. The entire town was out on Saturday and everyone saw her. Sometimes, she could barely stand up. At eight years old, I had a little boyfriend named Jerry Chastain. He was twelve. I think he had a ratty, banged up old bicycle that he used to run a paper route. His parents were severe alcoholics and would beat him up and take his money to buy more liquor. He was the sweetest, cutest little guy I ever knew. He had red, curly hair, big blue eyes, and lots of freckles. One Saturday, I was in the lobby of the Tropics waiting for my mother to bring me another quarter. He was passing by and saw me and came to the door of the lobby to speak to me. He said he was on his way to do his paper route but that he had a secret to tell me. He said he had a trick he was going to play on his parents to make them stop drinking. He would not tell me what he planned. Then he left. I looked up and here was my mother coming up the sidewalk, barely able to stand. I was so embarrassed.

About two days later, Jerry's brother, Charles, who was much older than Jerry, came by our house looking for Jerry. He had been missing for two days. I told him about my conversation with Jerry a couple of days before.

He said, "Okay. I'll keep looking for him."

He asked my father to please contact him if we saw or heard from Jerry. The next evening Charles came over again. You could tell the quiet young man was very upset and had been crying. He talked to Daddy outside. Then, they came inside, and Charles told me what had happened. They found Jerry hanging by a noose on the second floor, outside stairs. Yes, he was dead. He had hung there for three days and two nights, and his body had become elongated. I cried and cried and cried over him. He had once told me that we were going to get married when we were grown and that he would not drink alcohol. I will never forget him.

I met who was to become my best childhood friend. Her name was Beverly. We had a couple of other friends named Sally and Vicki. Beverly came from a large family of four girls and one boy. Her mama was really sweet but ruled the house. Her Daddy was a mean old bastard and drank two-quart bottles of Genesee beer every evening. He was a rude and mean drunk. I was eight years old when Mama started not being there. So, I would go to Beverly's after school, and her mother made sure I ate with them.

One evening, as I'm sitting at their table, her daddy asked her mother, "Who the hell is this little girl at my table? Don't she have a home to go to?"

Beverly's mom picked up a long handled, large wooden spoon and smacked him right out of his chair with it.

She told him, "Anyone I want to will eat at MY table. I work, too, and I cook the meal, so I say who can and can't eat. Watch yourself, old man."

I have never felt so very welcome in my life as her mother made me feel. In later years, I was able to tell her many things that had been going on as a child. Most of it she already knew. That's what happens when you live in a small town. Everyone knows your business and forms their own opinions, which are usually wrong.

Mama started going to the bar more often. She would disappear for two to three weeks at a time. Someone we didn't know would drop her off at home, and she would still be drunk. She would still be in the same clothes with piss and shit all over her, stumbling, and still drunk. How very disgusting. To this day, I can't stand the smell of beer on someone's breath.

Daddy would ask her, "Where have you been, Mildred?"

And mama would take an attitude and tell him, "I have been babysitting."

When we got home, Daddy had trouble opening the door. He finally pushed whatever was in the way out of the way.

Yeah, it was Mama. Drunk as hell and passed out on the floor in her own body fluids. Daddy left her there and told me to go to bed. I went to bed, crying, and finally fell asleep. The next day when I got up, Mama was already up and had showered and changed clothes and cleaned up her mess. It was as if nothing ever happened until the next time. This went on fairly frequently. Imagine, day after day, worrying about my mother. No one really discussed anything with me, so my fears constantly grew. Then when I was about 10 years old, she began bringing men home from the bar and calling them "boarders" and would make me give up my bedroom, and I had to sleep on the couch.

One of them, named Herbert, seemed nice enough. On a Saturday, Mama and Daddy went grocery shopping and left me in his care. He picked me up and put me on his lap, and I didn't fuss about it. I was so very hungry for love and affection that I liked it when he put his arms around me. You need to know that all my life my mother had told me I was the ugly duckling, and my sister was the beautiful princess. You hear that enough, and you begin to believe it. Anyway, he got a bit carried away, and began fondling me in all of my private areas. I got away from him and thought, "I'll just go ride my bicycle until Mama and Daddy get home."

While riding my bike, I fell off of it and broke my arm because I was so upset. No one had ever done something so strange to me, and I didn't like it. I knew it had to be wrong. I had fallen in front of a girl's house that I knew from school. She and her mother helped me up and out of the street. They picked up my bike out of the street, but it was so damaged I never got to ride it again. I told the girl's mother what had happened, and she said I was to stay there with them where it was safe until Mama and Daddy got home. This was just down the street, so we could see my house and would know when they got home. When they did get home the lady and her daughter took me and my bike home in their car. Mama and Daddy took me to the hospital to get my arm set in a cast. Then we went home and had dinner. I pulled Mama out to the back porch and told her what had happened. She said she would talk to Herbert.

A while later, Mama took me out to the back porch to talk to me.

"I talked to Herbert, and he said he was sorry and would not do it again," she said. "Don't tell your Daddy because he will kill him, and then your daddy will go to prison."

I didn't want my daddy to go to prison, so I held it in. Many years later when I told daddy about it, he began to cry.

"She was right about one thing," he said. "I would have killed the bastard."

I was 19 years old when I finally told him. Herbert left and then there were many others, and they would also molest me. I never said anything about the others because I thought no one would care. And so, I began to learn to keep my mouth shut and to suffer in silence. This was a period of time that was very difficult for me. Little did I know things were going to get worse.

There was a man I didn't know who would come to see Mama. She was not well. She spent a lot of time in bed. I didn't know why. I still don't know who this man was. One of her admirers I guess. I got the feeling that it had something to do with my sister. I didn't know until many years later that Mama had an affair with a man, and my sister was the result. Daddy raised her as his own though. Just as suddenly as he had appeared, the man disappeared. Didn't ever know his name.

We moved across the street when I was 10 years old. The house was a little bit bigger, which was nice. But it was the same neighborhood and the same town, and everybody knew us. Did anyone show me any consideration? No. I had a neighbor lady who kept telling me I would be just like my mother. You have no idea how angry that made me. I was taught to be respectful to my elders, but I was not respectful to her. When she would say that, I would scream at her that I was not my mother. My brothers and sister were out of there. They had no idea what was going on. And I never saw them to tell them.

Mama continued to get worse and worse, and I lost my mother. Everything continued to go wrong.

I had the mumps when I was about 10 or 11 years old and was having to sleep on the couch because we had a border. My bedroom was next to the living room, and I heard a lot of noises in my bedroom. So, being curious, I peeped through the keyhole. Here was my mother naked and in my bed with the border. He was at the foot of the bed and had his fist and his arm up to his elbow inside of my mother. Yes, that's what I said. I had never seen such a thing in my life and hope I never do again. I was very sick and running a fever, but I was not important.

You know when you are a little child you need a lot of love and atten-tion. I never got that. Men did not have much to do with little chil-dren back then. My father was a very quiet and private man. The only person I had to talk to was my best friend, Beverly, and my next-door neighbor Eugenia. Eugenia was about Mama's age, divorced, and had three daughters and one son. The son was my age, and he later mar-ried one of my friends, Patty.

Eugenia was always home. One day, Mama had left me a note to clean the kitchen. It was a very small kitchen. I had to melt the grease out of a cast iron skillet and drain it before I could wash it. I was not experienced as yet in the kitchen. The skillet was too heavy for me, and I dropped it on the floor. The hot grease went all over my legs and burned them badly. Eugenia heard me screaming and came to help me. She turned on the cold water in the tub and grabbed me and put me in it. The doctor said she saved me from worse damage. Mama was at the bar with the border, and Daddy was at work. I had to wait until someone got home to take me to the hospital. You could say that after about eight years of age, I was grossly neglected.

My poor father didn't know what to do. All of a sudden, when he was 60 years old, he had a 10-year-old little girl to finish raising and not a clue how to do it. He was born in 1901, and men did not raise children. We muddled through, somehow.

After we moved across the street, there were no more borders. I guess Daddy had enough of it. That's okay. Instead of borders, I be-came her target. One night I woke up because I couldn't breathe, I was choking, my throat and lungs seemed to be on fire. Imagine my surprise when I woke up and realized my mother was trying to choke me to death. Somehow, I got away from her and ran two blocks to Beverly's house. She opened the window and let me in, and the next morning, she loaned me clothes and shoes, so we could go to school. I soon learned this was to be a nightly problem. I would open my win-dow, undo the screen latch, and since the door had no lock I would push my bed against the door. That way, if mama started coming in, it would push the bed, I would feel it move, and quick like a bunny, I was out that window and running for my life. Almost every morning, Beverly's mom would notice me at their breakfast table and just wink her eye at me. I took from that that she understood why I was there, and it was okay. We never really talked about it until many years later.

Eventually, Daddy had to have her committed to the state mental facility in North Florida for the criminally insane because she kept trying to kill me. It was named Chattahoochee. Many years later, a cousin of mine was doing a family genealogy study and found that Mama's father had died there, as had his mother. This went on and on and on for many years. My grandmother and Aunt Etta would go to the hospital and sign her out and bring her back. What was the purpose? It happened again, over and over. The doctors diagnosed her as a paranoid schizophrenic with homicidal tendencies. She was also an alcoholic. At fifteen years old, I was beginning to have my own problems due to all this. I had begun to sink into madness. I put blankets over my windows so it would be black inside, just like my heart felt. I saw spiders crawling on the walls, huge spiders, but of course, there were none. I began retreating from the world. I didn't have anything to do with my friends, didn't eat or sleep, and just stayed in my room. Mama went off on a drunk, and was gone about three weeks. I had gone to bed for the night when she came home, as usual, still drunk and stinking and bodily fluids on her.

Obviously, I was not in a good frame of mind. Something that added to that was the results of a party I went to.

A friend of mine asked me to be the blind date for a guy that was returning from serving 18 months in Vietnam. Every guy we knew was either in Vietnam, died there, or came home. Most of the ones that came home were damaged, either physically or mentally. I was fifteen years old, and my oldest brother was in Vietnam, so I said okay. My friend Marsha was eighteen years old and had a car. The party was out of town, and Marsha's father came to my father and got permission for me to come and stay with them for a couple of weeks since it was summer. No one was home with me during the daytime. We went to the party and knew most of the people there. I was astounded by the home. Remember, I was very poor and thought plastic drapes put us up there with the Rockefeller's. There were huge, crystal chandeliers, thick carpets, embossed wall paper, etc. It was almost unbelievable! I met my date. He was blond, tall, and very well-built after eighteen months in the jungle. I had not known him before. It turned out that he was a lot older than me. He was twenty-six years old. He saw my reaction to his grandma's home. The party was held there because his grandma was in Europe for the summer.

He asked me, "Would you like to have a look around?"

I nodded yes, so off we went.

The last bedroom he showed me was his grandmother's. I stepped one foot inside and that's when he pushed me inside and locked the door. I knew I was in trouble. He wouldn't let me out and threw me onto the bed, and he followed. I weighed about 100 pounds, and he was very muscular and strong at about 200 pounds. Not much of a match. He began to tear my clothes open. I screamed for help.

Soon, I could hear friends trying to get in the door. Meanwhile, he began to fight with me. I thought, He's going to rape me.

That piece of crap! I was still a virgin and that seemed to excite him even more. I had my legs crossed at the knee and at the ankles. He tore my clothes down the middle, then punched me in the face. I tried to swing on him, but he caught my fist in his hand and laughed.

"I will take your cherry," he said. "That will teach you to play with the big boys."

The fight continued. He kept hitting me, and I kept trying to fight him. My friends were banging on the door and yelling at me to "hang in there, we're coming." I decided I needed some major help, so I began to pray inside my head. The answer I got was scary. My inner voice said, Kill him, kill him now, or he will kill you.

I don't know where the strength came from except from God and adrenaline. I put my hands on his throat, dug in with my fingers, and proceeded to rip his throat out. He collapsed onto me and bled out on top of me. He was dead weight, and I couldn't get him off of me. I was beyond hysterical, and my friends finally got the door off the hinges and came in. No one could believe what they saw. The guys got him off of me. The girls wrapped me in sheets as my clothes were destroyed. We moved out to the living room. Everyone was scared now. One of the girls called the police. We didn't have 911 emergency then. Nobody knew what to do. I was still hysterical. I had killed a man, albeit under God's direction, and I didn't know the law. My daddy always told me that if you killed in self-defense, you would be okay. But I wondered what they would think of me.

The cops arrived, and they were guys that were from our town, and Marsha had gone to school with them. They wanted to know if he had managed to rape me.

I told them, "NO, I managed to kill him before he could ruin me."

They asked if I needed or wanted to go to the hospital. I told them no. Then when they got my last name, they got quiet.

"Are you David's daughter or William's?"

I told them I was William's daughter.

"Oh, hell," they said. "Are you going home tonight, or are you staying with someone?"

Marsha told them I was staying with her for the next two weeks. Most of the bruises would be gone, and the cuts from him punching me would be healed or almost healed by the time I went home.

The cops finally told all of us, "You can go but do not tell anyone about this. He deserved to die. All through high school and after, this guy had been charged with rape on several occasions. His family was wealthy and always bought off the victim. This time it didn't work. We'll take care of things. All of you go home."

Marsha called her mom and told her what happened and that I was hysterical and could not stop crying. We left, as did everyone else. When we got to Marsha's, her mom was waiting for us. Very quietly, as we didn't want to wake up her father, we went to Marsha's room. Her mom gave me a strong pain pill and a nerve pill and climbed in the shower with me. She managed to peel my ruined clothing off of me and bathed me. She washed the blood out of my hair. She got me dried off and helped me into some pajamas of Marsha's. I began to calm down and went to sleep. Marsha told me the next day that after I went to sleep, her mom made her tell what happened. Her mom told her that she and Marsha would take good care of me, and hopefully, I would be healed or almost healed when I went home. I didn't tell Daddy about it until many years later.

"You did the right thing," he said. "Don't worry about it."

The weird part was that there was nothing in the papers or the local news about him. It was as if he never really existed. But I didn't forget about it, and then mother started with her problems again.

I had left home in late September. At Thanksgiving, we went to Leesburg. My brother-in-law and my niece stayed with his family, and my sister and I stayed with Mama and Daddy. Mama was acting very strange again.

I told my sister, "She's getting ready to go off again."

None of my family believed me about mother and how dangerous she was. I got the distinct feeling something really bad was going to happen. Daddy had surgery for a long-time problem with an abdominal hernia. Mother came over from Grandma's to take care of him. Why would you send a paranoid schizophrenic with homicidal tendencies to take care of someone after surgery? He might have been better off if a cobra had taken care of him.

On the Monday after Thanksgiving, my sister and I felt worried, teary-eyed, and on edge. We knew something was wrong. That evening we got a call from Daddy. That morning, he had asked Mama for a second cup of coffee. She went and got his hammer instead and beat in the front and top of his head. Then, she threw him on the ground and tried to choke him. He was tall and thin, but strong. Mama was short but very strong. She tried to choke him to death, but he got away and ran next door to his friend's house. Daddy had white, silver hair, and when his friend's wife opened the door and saw Daddy, she nearly had a heart attack. She got Daddy inside and locked the door, then called to her husband, who was outside working in his garden. He was an old railroad engineer and always strapped on a .45cal pistol each morning out of habit. He came in and saw Daddy. His wife had called for an ambulance and had put ice in a towel and was holding it to Daddy's head. Her husband said it would take too long, so he put Daddy in his car and drove him to the emergency room. He had to have over 130 stitches to close his head. The police were called. At home, Mama had gotten a knife and headed across the street to Eugenia's.

She told Eugenia that she "hadn't been doing right."

Eugenia and her little girl took off up the street to the convenience store where she called and reported it to the police. Mama walked downtown and went over to the cab company, where she had worked as a dispatcher at one time. She asked to use the bathroom, which she did then disappeared. The owner, Smitty, knew of mother's problems. He had just sharpened a lot of large knives and had them on a table near the bathroom. He went back to check on her and found that she and the knives were all gone. He called the police. This was more calls than the police usually received.

The police chief was Slim Perry. He knew us and our family. He went looking for Mama and found her on a side street. He pulled up and asked if she needed a ride. Mama gave him the knives and got into the car. She was taken to a neighboring town where the hospital had a psychiatric ward. The next day, she was taken back to Chattahoochee without a chance of release. For the next 10 years or so, she was moved around to other state facilities that were for geriatric patients.

When my niece was four years old, she decided she wanted to live with her daddy. She pointed out that her "mommy was never home," and that "only Aunt Gloria was ever with her." That "only Aunt Gloria cared about her." So, she went back to St. Petersburg to live with her father. My sister only wanted to go to work, come home for dinner, then go out to the Coral Lounge, which was about the only "hot spot" around.

I dated some. On Tuesday nights, we did laundry and would hang out at Dottie's Chicken Shack, a local hangout. There were usually drag races at the old airport. It was a blast! Remember, this was during the muscle car era. Every guy I knew had a Mustang, a Mustang Fastback, GTO, Super B, and so on. I learned a lot about cars. That way, they would let me hang around.

He said, "I know the Mustang was a piece of shit, but it was my piece of shit!"

I met a guy named Tony that I had seen around town. He and I dated for two-and-a-half years, and he was my first love. He has passed on at this date in time. At the end of that school year, my sister gave me three days' notice that she and her husband were getting back together. Her belly was getting a little big, and she said her uterus was tipped out of place.

What did I know? I was 17 and basically deserted. I wasn't even offered the chance to go back to Daddy's. I rented a room at a boarding house and got a waitress job for the summer. Before the end of summer, I got really sick. Probably because I ate a meal at work and a lot of boiled peanuts. A couple of elderly ladies lived across the street from the boarding house. One day, I was so sick I managed to lurch across the street and ask to use their phone. They saw how sick I was and let me call Lois, my boyfriend's mother. They helped me get back to the boarding house. Lois and her little girl, Kara, came and got me.

She took me home with them and took care of me. She had been a nurse, so she knew what to do.

I was having trouble with the arch in one of my feet. Tony took me to the doctor and he gave me a shot in my arch that hurt like hell. It burned badly, and I started crying and couldn't stop. The doctor gave me a shot of Thorazine. Tony had to carry me to the car and then inside at his mother's.

All I did was sleep the next 36 hours. Tony's mother said that one time she came in to check on me, and I had no heartbeat and wasn't breathing. I knew when she meant. I had a near-death experience where I was going down a black tunnel with a white light at the end. The closer I got to the light, the faster I traveled.

Then, I heard a voice say, "Not now. It's too soon."

After that, I started coming back to myself and woke up. Thank God for Lois and for Tony. He was great to me. I had never had anyone treat me so well. I will always love him. I'm the one that screwed things up. He never spoke to me again.

I started my senior year at high school, and Lois's oldest son came home from serving in Korea in the Army. One night, I was off work and was home at Lois's. Tony was at work. He was a professional musician, and one of the best. His brother, David, lied and told Tony that he and I had sex while he was gone. Not so. He was just angry because the virgin he had been engaged to had broken off with him. No one wanted to believe me, so I had to move back into town to an old apartment that my sister and I had once lived in. It was $50 a month, water included, but no electric the first few months. Then, I lost my job and wasn't at school.

Two of my teachers found out where I lived and came to see about me. They got me a part-time job at the post office. It paid well enough that I only had to work part-time. Tony began coming to see me again. He knew I hadn't cheated on him. I don't remember why, but I lost my job at the post office, so I went back to work at the restaurant. It was March or April now. My grades were Bs and As. I moved in with another girl to cut my bills down. I began to get sick and then rented a room from a friend. It got so that I didn't go to school or work, and I don't remember a lot except I would cry for Tony. He would come by after work to see me.

One day, I looked up, and my father was standing by my bed, crying. Lois had driven to Leesburg and got Daddy. They loaded me up in her car and took me home. Keep in mind, we had no phone or car, so it took concerted effort on her part to find him. I never knew how she did find him. Anyway, Lois took us to the doctor's.

When I got in to see the doctor, he told Daddy he would have his nurse call Waterman Memorial in Eustis to see if they had a bed open for me. I raised all kinds of hell. I shouted at the doctor that they would have to "rope and hog-tie me to get me there."

The doctor told Daddy that if I had that much spirit left, he needed to take me home, try to get me to eat, let me sleep as much as I wanted, and not tell me what to do. So, Lois took us home and then left for her own home. When we got home, my mother was there. Not a good choice. Not by a longshot.

One day, I got up about 11 a.m. and went out to the kitchen. Here came Mama through the back door with a beer in a brown paper sack turned up to get all of it. I lost it!

I started screaming at her.

"Damn you! You're the reason I'm like I am! A damned nervous breakdown at 18 years of age. I can't take you anymore! Get out!"

I think I went back to bed.

When I woke up, she was gone. I didn't even hear my aunt come to get her. Daddy and I did not discuss it.

Meanwhile, Juanita, the convenience store clerk, close friend, an avid romantic said there was a really cute guy that came in every day that I "just had to meet." She told me to come up in the afternoon. A few days later, I did. He came in, and WOW! We became immediate best friends, and he included me with his two friends. We hung out together, made wonderful love together, went to his dad's church.

Oh! Did I leave that out?

His dad was a minister. He had been shot in the face in WWII and had no smell or taste or sight. But he was as sweet as my daddy was. His mother was a large woman, not at all fat, just tall and big-boned, like I am. His sister, Becky, still had baby fat on her, but she was equally sweet. We all liked each other really well. He introduced me to them almost as soon as we met.

Daddy liked Mac a lot better than he did Tony. Tony was Native American and dark, plus he wouldn't talk to Daddy. Mac had "run at the mouth" sometimes, but he was always friendly and happy. He did a lot for my healing. I think he may be a minister somewhere. I know about six months later, they had to move to Jacksonville to another church. He also had an older brother who was a minister there. Never heard from him again.

When I felt better, I got a job waitressing at the Rexall Drug Store. I knew I needed to help Daddy with the bills. One Sunday, I was in the process of making chicken and dumplings when a strange car pulled up. It was my oldest brother, Gene, with a new wife. She was from Massachusetts, and we southerners could barely understand her.

We just thought they came for a visit. Surprise. After dinner, Daddy went into the living room to read the Sunday paper and left me in the kitchen. Gene told me to pack my things because I was coming with them. I didn't know anything about it. I thought Daddy had written him to come get me. I didn't know. I found out many, many years later that when Loretta had visited a couple of months before she saw me take a prescription tranquilizer. It was in the pharmacy bottle. She was so uneducated that she called Gene and told him I was a drug addict, and he needed to go get me. I am not, nor have I ever been a drug addict. Never will be either. I don't believe a person should not be in control of themselves, their actions, or the results of others actions against them.

We had the car loaded, and I went to say goodbye to Daddy. We had walked right past him when loading the car. But, I'm afraid my father had long ago chosen to ignore a lot of things that were going on. I guess it was just his way of coping. I wish I had known then what it took me years to realize. I loved my father very much and would not have hurt him for anything.

Anyway, away we went to North Carolina. My brother was a sergeant in the Marine Corps in charge of Motor T in Camp LeJeune. It was beautiful up there. He lived off base in a rural area. The nearest town was Newport, and I began school in Morehead City. I liked it. Everyone I met, anywhere, was really nice. I made more friends than I had ever had. My best friend was Dawn.

One Sunday, she borrowed the car, and we went to hang out at Atlantic Beach, which was nearby. It was winter—November, to be exact, and the wind was blowing in off the Atlantic. We were walking up and down the beach as were two young Marines. We passed each other a couple of times and then they said hello. They invited us to take a ride in the other guy's car. His name was Buddy, and he was from Tennessee. The one that seemed interested in me was named Fred. We had a couple of beers with them and exchanged phone numbers and went home.

I had a 5 p.m. curfew on Sundays, and we started dating. He swept me off my feet. He was from Florida, though he originally grew up in Pennsylvania. Mama warned me about those "Yankee men," but we fell in love very quickly and forcefully. Gene and Claire didn't like him. Then again, Claire didn't like anyone. He had to leave for Tech School in Whidbey Island, Washington. He would be gone until late February. We wrote each other, and he called when he could. I found out I was pregnant, and so was my cat. He called me and said he got my letter telling him that my cat was pregnant, and so was someone else.

He asked, "Are you pregnant?"

I said, "Yes."

He said, "Well, we talked about getting married after you graduate in June. You want to go ahead and get married now?"

I was a little unsure but said, "okay."

A few days after his call, I came out of the bathroom after another morning sickness episode.

Gene's wife asked, "What is wrong with you? You've been throwing up an awful lot."

I told her she must be stupid because, obviously, I was pregnant. All kinds of hell broke loose. No one asked who the father was, what our plans were—nothing. They both erupted in anger at me. My brother kicked me out and said he wasn't going to take the blame for it. He said I had to leave.

I went to school and talked to one of my friends who was married. They let you go to school there even if you were married and/or pregnant. She and I went to my brother's while he was at work. We packed up my stuff, and I went home with her, including my cat. I stayed about a week, sleeping on her couch. Her husband and I didn't like each other.

I was still going to school. First semester exams were coming up. I didn't want to miss them. I was a straight A student and wanted to get credit for that semester. A couple of my guy friends lived with three college guys on Atlantic Beach and invited me to stay with them since my friend's husband was so unfriendly. I moved in with them and slept on the couch.

I'll tell you, no weather in Florida prepared me for the bone-aching chill that came off the Atlantic, and they were right on the beach. I only had one blanket, and one night the college guys started calling out that I could sleep with them.

I said, "No way in hell!"

Then my friend Ernie told me to come to him, and demanded the other guys back off and leave me alone. I climbed in bed with him. We were both fully dressed and rolled up in the two blankets to stay warm. We did stay warm and slept well, then it was up and off to school as usual. He and I stayed friends for a long time. I cooked and cleaned for them, and they moaned when I left to go home for Christmas.

I went home and had a nice visit at Christmas. I didn't know yet that I was pregnant. I had a nice surprise. My brother Ed had been paroled from Leavenworth Prison to Daddy. I hadn't seen him in years. We all had a great time. It was after I returned from Christmas that I found out I was pregnant.

I took my first semester exams with no problem. Right after that is when the scene took place at my brother's. I finally got the money together and went home in January. It was probably a few days before I told Daddy. I was so afraid to tell him. When I told him, he told me there were girls out there that had sex with a different man every night, and he knew I wasn't one of them. He said he would stand beside me, whatever my decision was. I told him we planned to marry.

He said, "Okay," then asked, "Do you love Fred?"

I said, "Yes."

Daddy said, "Well, it's either marriage, or give the baby up for adoption."

I told him I loved my baby and would not give it up for adoption. Abortion was legal in a few states, and my sister lived in one of them. There is no way I would have aborted him. I only believe it should be done in cases of rape, incest, or if the mother or child's life is in danger. Certainly not as a means of birth control, as it seems to be used now. And, I do believe it is a woman's right to decide.

I got a temporary job as a personal maid. The lady I worked for was very nice, and she really liked the job I did. She knew I was pregnant and working to buy my wedding dress and outfit. She would make me stop for an hour and have me eat a large, healthy lunch, which was very nice of her. Fred was going to his parent's around February 22.

He came to meet my father and stayed the night. Daddy talked to him about many things, I am sure. Daddy had been a Marine and had guarded the President of the United States in the oval office in the 1920s. He took an oath not to tell who it was, and he took that oath to his grave. He also let Fred know that in my family, the women are not to be hit or mistreated.

He told him, "I may be an old man, but I've been swinging a hammer all my life. I reckon I could do you in if you hit my baby girl."

I guess he listened, somewhat. He didn't hit me until many years later.

I went to see Lois. Tony had married at the beginning of December and wouldn't even speak to me. She and Kara helped me make my veil. I bought an ice blue dress with a V-neck and fairly straight skirt. It was street length. I also bought a pair of white heels to wear. Daddy bought my bride's bouquet for me; it was a beautiful white orchid with small white roses and baby's breath. I cried because it was so beautiful. Aunt Etta paid for the altar flowers, which were also white orchids. She also paid for a lady Lois knew to make the wedding cake. It was beautiful. Grandma paid for a tasteful, old-fashioned reception of cake, punch, mints, and nuts. Lois was my Matron of Honor and my flower girls, in pale yellow, were Kara and Cathy, Ed's girlfriend's daughter. It was very nice and small and took place in my Grandma's church in Coleman, Florida. I always said I was going to get married in my Grandma's church, and I did.

We stayed our wedding night at the Big Bass Motel in Leesburg. Ed had tied tin cans to the bumper of our car. Fred's father had bought us a '62 Pontiac as a wedding gift. The next day, we went to my daddy's early and packed all the wedding gifts. Thanks to the women in grandma's church and relatives, we only had to buy a mop, broom, and garbage can to set up housekeeping. Another life began for me.

I got up at 5:30 a.m. to cook Fred's breakfast. I would put on the coffee and bacon and go throw up. I would turn the bacon, then go throw up. Put on the eggs, then go throw up. Fred said I cured him of early morning breakfasts. He started letting me sleep and went to the commissary on base for breakfast. Our first home was an 8x38 foot mobile home. It actually had two bedrooms. You could sit on the toilet, brush your teeth, and wash your feet in the shower. Boy, was it small. Our monthly income back then (1971) was $236 per month. Our rent was $85 a month. I budgeted our money and planned my menu. I gave us $36 each of two paydays for food. One of the few compliments he gave me was he didn't know how I kept us on budget and made three good meals a day, plus desserts and snacks. He said I was the only person who could get two delicious meals out of one scrawny-assed chicken. Then, I found the egg farm in town and was able to buy a flat of 25 eggs for 25 cents. We ate a lot of eggs.

After about three months, he began to show his true self. I found I didn't like him very much anymore. Every day, he would come home and start screaming at me, jumping up and down, cussing, and hitting the walls and the refrigerator. I made sure my cast iron skillet and butcher knife Daddy gave me were nearby. A southern girl is taught to use those to defend herself if necessary from an abusive husband. I was too young to realize that even though he wasn't hitting me, he was psychologically and mentally abusing me less than a year since my nervous breakdown. I really loved it when he told me to go "fuck myself." I had never been talked to like that in my entire life! Now I was being disrespected every single day.

He wanted sex every single night. I was 19, and I came from a very conservative family. His family drank alcohol all the time. I was only around my mother's drunkenness. There was no alcohol in our home except for medicinal purposes.

I wrote home frequently but did not mention his behavior. My father would have been very upset. I figured I could handle it myself. We went home a couple of times a year, but I never got to spend any time with my daddy. We always stayed at his parent's home in Indian

Rocks Beach, about an hour and a half away. They made more money and had a nicer home. I was very upset about it, but what was I to do? Fred was not a very communicative person and cussed a lot. I didn't like it.

Some of the single guys on Cherry Point, North Carolina, station would come to our house. They found out I could cook. On payday, about 4 o'clock, they would begin to arrive with four or five chickens and bags of potatoes. It was fun. They would peel the potatoes and cut them up to make mashed potatoes, and I had taught the guys that at the base the chickens were 10 cents a pound less if you cut it up yourself. I had to teach them how to cut it up. Then I would fry chicken for what seemed like forever. They would hang around and visit, and I usually went to bed before they left.

My pregnancy was okay, I guess. I threw up several times a day until two weeks before my child arrived. I woke up one morning in mild labor, so we went to the base to the doctor, and he sent me home for things to get moving along. My landlady, Mrs. Smith, lived across the street and I knew in her 40 years as a Marine Corps wife, she had helped many young wives that were pregnant. We left Fred at home, and she and I walked all around the neighborhood and introduced me to a lot of non-military neighbors that lived nearby. I remembered when my mother had told me that when I went into labor to start walking a lot. It would help the labor to move along.

At first, my pains were not regular, then they went to one every four minutes. We headed back home. It was a couple of blocks. By the time we got there, my pains were two minutes apart.

Fred tried to get me to eat. No, you never eat when you're in labor.

Anyway, we left for the hospital. It was 10 miles away. By the time we got there, the pains were right on top of each other. My water had not broken, so they gave me some medicine to slow it down. Back then, civilian hospitals did not allow fathers into the labor room or delivery.

But on a military base, if the husband was in country, then he had to be with his wife during her labor and right after. They finally broke my water, and we were told it would be a few more hours. WRONG! It was maybe 15 minutes later, and I was coming straight out of the bed. They put all of us women in large Navy shirts for this part. Fred picked up my shirt and took a look. Then he went out to the doctor.

He asked, "Hey, Dr. Gardner, when do you know it's time for delivery?"

Doc said, "When you can see the top of their head."

Fred said, "What about when you can see their ears?"

The doctor threw his paperwork in the air and yelled for the nurse. Off we went to delivery. We got in there, and the doc was trying to put a saddle block into my spine so I wouldn't feel pain. Really? My child was already out half-way up his ears! By the fifth try, I told the doc to either get it this time or forget it! This baby was coming.

I had been sitting on the side of the gurney. I wasn't aware but shift changed for the corpsmen. They were like LPNs. They turned me around, and the corpsman began padding my leg stirrups and my legs. I looked up at him and nearly died of embarrassment. I was a very modest person, and this was killing me. Anyway, I looked at the corpsman and realized he was one of our friends, named Jeff. He was from Wisconsin and very funny.

I just about died right there! I have never been so embarrassed. I think I said something like, "Oh, my God, no! It's Jeff."

He smiled and spoke, "Don't worry, honey, I'm here to help."

I started crying. Our son was born at 8:47 p.m. on a Thursday night. He was a skinny guy, but very long. He came down the birth canal screaming.

Doc looked at me and said, "You're going to have your hands full with this one."

I always thought he was just hungry. Back then, they took the baby away immediately to assess them and clean them up. Then I got to hold him a few minutes.

He was taken to the nursery, and I was taken to my room. I shared the room with a black girl. She had given birth to a little girl about three minutes after me. We had no air conditioning, and it was August. Fred brought in a fan for us. Only the labor and delivery rooms were air conditioned. That was the government's way of saving money I guess. We had a nurse's call bell for 12 hours—if we woke up before then. The call bell went away and whether you awoke before 12 hours or at 12 hours; that was all the coddling you got. Then, the nurse would stand you up and check you out for signs of hemorrhaging, take your vitals, and so on. After that, they showed you the communal bathroom and communal sitz bath room. We were taught to disinfect the toilet even, before and after we used it. It was the same for the sitz bath and the showers. I guess that's how they keep the moms from getting infected.

Then we got a meal. Since my roommate and I were both breast feeders, our corpsman would bring us enough food to feed three people. The tray would have so much food and fluids on it, I couldn't eat it all. I silently wondered if he swiped them from the Officer's Mess because we had steak about twice a day.

There were no phones or TVs.

When my little boy came to me, I held him tight. I have never loved anyone so much in my life. It was truly a blessed day when he was born. We had picked out all kinds of girl names, but hadn't planned for a boy. Fred was a Junior, but I didn't want our son to be "the third." He was named Jason, and his middle name was my maiden name. I wanted to carry on my family name. I didn't even want to take my husband's name. I was not one of them. I was my own person. I did not want to lose my identity. My father told me to take my husband's name as it was traditional, and he wouldn't have our family shamed by such action. So, I had a different name from my family.

Gloria Leigh Wilhite

At first, Fred seemed like the proud papa. He bought cigars and bragged at work about his son. We came home on a Saturday morning. Mrs. Smith came over to meet the new little one. Friends asked if we needed anything. All we needed was a baby book and a diaper pail, so they got them for us. That was a good thing about the Corps, people were nice; you had friends, and we had our own rules and behavior to follow. Just to show you, Fred had once told me that if I was on base without him and something happened and I needed help, to look around for the most stripes or look for an officer.

"DON'T try to handle it yourself," he said.

One day, I was on base for what we called "cattle call." This was when only pregnant women had appointments to check our vitals and our urine, if we were having any problems or not, we would see a doctor. Afterwards, I would go to the commissary and have a sandwich and drink before driving home. I had that appointment and then went to the commissary. I was walking past a bunch of young non-coms, mostly privates and privates first-class. One of them, a real asshole, thought it would be funny to trip me. I caught myself before hitting the floor. I was about to knock the shit out of him, then I remembered that Marines are responsible for their spouse's behavior on board base. So, I looked around, and lo and behold, there was a full-bird colonel. He was having a cup of coffee and reading the paper. I went over to him with tears of anger, but I acted like a poor little girl who needed help. You could tell I was pregnant, and the majority of men showed great respect for such things.

I gently coughed to get his attention, and he looked up, saw the tears, jumped up, and came to attention.

"How can I help you Ma'am?"

I cried, letting a few tears fall. I wasn't sad; I was highly pissed. He didn't need to know that. I told him one of those young men had tripped me, and I didn't think he should be allowed to do that. He could have hurt me and my baby. The colonel wanted to know if I was

34

okay or if I needed to go to the hospital. I told him I was okay that I had been able to catch myself. He got red in the face, set me down in a chair and got me a glass of water, then he went over to the young man I pointed out. He stripped him of rank and his chevrons. The last I saw the guy he was being hauled off by the MPs for the brig. I loved it. I felt I was home again. That's how the men in my family would have handled it, after beating him half to death. I love men who have respect for the women who carry, birth, and raise the next generation.

Then, the colonel came back to me, all calmed down and got info on who my husband was and what company he was with. Then, I went home. Fred was late getting home that evening, but when he got home he came in and said, "Jesus Christ, Gloria! What did you do?"

That made me angry. He acted like I did something wrong. I told him what happened, and I followed his instructions.

He said, "All I know is my top sent me to see some colonel. I went there, and he shook my hand and poured me a glass of good scotch and told me what happened and how he handled it."

He said the Colonel had not only stripped the guy of rank, but gave him 30 days in the brig to think about it. One of his charges was the inevitable charge of "Actions unbecoming of a Marine." I loved it.

I thought that maybe we would be a little better together now. I had given him a son, and he seemed proud of that. Boy, was I wrong! He gave Jason a bottle one time, when my milk started slowing down. I let Jason tell me when he was hungry. That was about every 2 hours. It was exhausting. That was the only help I got from him. My lady neighbors came over each day after Fred left for work and would clean, bring casseroles, and such. They'd give me a break, so I could get a shower or a nap. They were wonderful.

Then, Fred would get home and the shit would start.

Imagine every day starting with a beautiful little baby to care for all day and spending such loving time with them. Then, you keep the house clean, and get the laundry done, and a make nice meal each evening, just so you get screamed at and cussed at when your "loving" husband gets home. The only saving factor was that we had a lot of company from the base. Fred didn't yell and punch walls or the refrigerator when we had company.

We had an American breed German Shepard. He was a good dog with a bad habit of getting into the outside garbage can. He did this one day when Jason had only been home for a few days. Fred flipped his wig and threw the dog inside the garbage can and put the lid on. Then, he rolled it up and down the dirt road beating on it with a stick and screaming cuss words. I think I learned a few new ones. My landlady came over and wanted to know if Fred had finally flipped out. When he and the dog finally came home, I told him if he didn't get some psychiatric help, I was going to leave him.

The next day, he let the dog out to use the bathroom, and he never came home.

Would you? Being treated like that!

Fred cried and looked all over for him. No one had seen him. Imagine that. He did go for some help a couple of times. He played handball with a colonel at the gym on base for a short time, and that was it.

Fred loved his sex. The doctor told him, as they do every new father, to wait 6 weeks before having sex again after childbirth. Three, yes, three weeks after our son was born, he raped me.

Now, you may say, "Well, he's your husband, he should be able to have sex whenever he wants it."

Well, I'll tell you what: a man made that rule. And thank God, in the early 1970s, they made it a law that a woman had a right to refuse her husband. After all, it is her body. We went to bed one night, and he mentioned it, and I said no. So, he proceeded to hold me forcefully down and put his hand over my mouth as I started to scream. Then he jammed his way into me. There was no love there. He was brutal, and forceful, and that was rape.

God, how I began to hate him and lose all respect for him. I thought I had to bear it and follow my wedding vows. I went in for my six-week check-up, and my doctor had a fit.

He yelled at me, "Do you want another baby right away?"

I looked at him and said, "Hell no! I don't want another baby with him at all! My husband held me down and took me by force."

He said he could help me with the unwanted pregnancy. He left the room and came back with five very strong birth control pills and had me take them all at once. He said I should get my regular period in seven to 10 days, and if I didn't, he told me to come back and request him, and he would do a D&C to clean me out. I got my period in the seven days. I also went on birth control pills for a year and then changed to a different form of birth control.

Fred finally saw my temper. I have a very bad temper, and I had really had enough. One day a few weeks after Jason was born, I was hanging diapers on the clothesline. He came out and said to me, "I'm going to take the baby to my mom to raise."

I guess he had never pissed off a mother before. My home was clean; the baby was clean and well cared for. He had no reason to threaten me like that. It got my back up, just like a mama cat.

I told him, "You even try to take him anywhere, and I will kill you. It's just that simple, so you better listen up."

He never tried that again. I soon found that Fred was a bully. Well, I'll tell you what, I don't cotton to bullies and never have.

When Jason was three months old, I had just fed him and was getting his bath ready. Fred starts dancing around with him on his shoulders. I told him not to because it would cause the baby to throw up on him. Did he listen? Of course not. Typical male, hard-headed and stubborn. Soooo, you guessed it. He threw up ground meat, spinach, macaroni and cheese, and applesauce. Oh yeah, I almost forgot about the special effects the milk had in the whole thing. I couldn't help it, but I started laughing, and Fred didn't like to be laughed at.

He had no real sense of humor. Poor Jason, Fred grabbed him off his shoulders and handed him to me.

He said, "You clean him up, I'm getting a shower."

That was the beginning and the end of Fred paying attention to Jason while he was a baby. No matter how much I tried to get Fred to play with Jason and his toys or blocks, he just wouldn't.

My oldest brother had become a friend again. He lived nearby on 10 acres of land. He had divorced Claire and was dating a lady who lived in Swansboro. He moved in with her and offered to rent us his home. We took him up on it. It was much nicer, had A/C, and was in a nice, rural area.

We lived right on the main road between Newport and the base. It was exactly nine miles from the Baptist Church to the front gates of the base. It was aptly named Nine Mile Road. How about that, clever. We had a new German Shepard, a stocky, German breed. There was a farmer who owned property just behind us, and he grew soy beans and peanuts in that field. After harvest, he left some in the fields and turned his hogs loose to fatten up before sending them to market. Our dog, Keiser, used to jump the fence and chase the hogs around. When the farmer came to check on them, he would scratch his head trying to figure out why the hogs were losing weight instead of gaining. Ha.

One of Fred's best friends, Leon, from California used to spend a lot of time with us. Most weekends and holidays. Sometimes even during the week. He used to call Jason his "little buddy." I was very drawn to him. I don't know how he and Fred had ever become friends. They were so different. Both liked to smoke a little weed or have a little wine and a good time. We would cook out, have dinners, go out for pizza; he paid for all three of us to go to New Bern to see The Godfather: Part I, and he paid for pizza afterwards. We would go to the beach, and when he saw how Fred ignored his son, then he would pick Jason up and take him out to the waves. We stayed up late many nights playing cards. One time, Fred asked me if Leon and I had ever had sex.

I said, "What do you think?"

He never asked again. I thought he knew that no matter what a bastard he was, I wasn't going to cheat on him. From the way he acted after that, I don't think he believed me. I have always heard that people will think the worst unless you set them straight. I believe it. I set him straight, but I don't think he believed me.

Sort of an odd situation began to unfold. A friend of mine from high school days, Ernie, worked not far from where we lived. He passed our house on his way home from work. He began stopping in right at dinner time. I didn't mind. I always made enough for one or two more people. Just a good rule of thumb. Especially if you're in the military. He would stay for dinner and then go home and get cleaned up and come back about when I had put the baby down, and we would watch television and visit. It got so that every night a different additional guy would come over.

On a Saturday night, Fred had taken the only car and gone out somewhere. I didn't care. I had a break from him at least. Ernie showed up, and no one else came over. Leon and I were still talking, and he wanted me to leave Fred and marry him. I was seriously considering it. Anyway, I finally asked Ernie if I could ask him a question. He said sure.

I asked, "Why is someone over here every night? I mean, I don't mind. I like the company. And, Fred behaves himself if you all are here."

He answered me with a very stern face, "You think he's bad at home, you should see him out with us. We are checking to see if you or the baby have any marks on you. If we ever see any, he will disappear. We will kill him, cut him into pieces, and within 12 hours or less, his pieces will be in the deep woods in 3 states. They'll never find him. If that happens, all you will really know is that he is missing. You wait 2 days and call the Provost Marshall on the base and tell them he's missing. They'll take care of you and Jason."

Wow! I knew I wasn't the only person who didn't like him very well, but DAMN! I wasn't quite ready for that. Oh well, that was karma. But, of course, Fred was smart enough to know not to ever hit me or Jason. I would have cleaned his clock, so to speak. I have a great cast iron skillet that my daddy's breakfasts were cooked in all his life. I also had an "Old Hickory" butcher knife that my daddy had sharpened before he gave it to me as a wedding gift. Maybe he knew something I didn't.

When Mama and Daddy got married they lived in Savannah Beach, Georgia, during WWII, and they would go out jukin' on the weekend. Daddy made good money building ships for the Navy. He was a master carpenter and a shipwright.

It seems daddy liked his whiskey, but it turned him mean. He would beat the crap out of my mama. This was when Mama only had the 2 boys. Anyway, after one of many beatings, Mama told Daddy not to ever hit her again or he would regret it. The very next weekend, it happened again. So, true to her word, Mama made good on all her threats. Mama waited for him to pass out. When he did, she got down his razor strop, which was leather, tied his hands to the headboard, and his feet to the footboard. Then she began to beat the living hell out of him. My oldest brother was about 11 years old when he witnessed this for himself and stayed the hell out of it. At some point, Daddy regained momentary consciousness and tried to get loose. But, mama had him tied tight. She kept on beating. My brother said blood flew off of Daddy. When she was through she left Daddy where he was and packed a suitcase for her and the boys and got on a bus.

They made it to Jacksonville, Florida. Mama had to put the boys in an orphanage, but only to keep, never to adopt. Mama got a waitress job and would take money to the orphanage for their care. Daddy told me the same story. He said he quit drinking, and he laid there for 3 days before his boss came looking for him. He said he was in bad shape, but he said he deserved it and to never let a man hit me and get away with it.

My brother Ed, and his girlfriend and her little boy had lived at my brother Gene's before us. One day, Joann shot herself in the stomach with a repeating rifle. It jammed after five shots. Fred and Leon had gone over there to work on their cars. My brother Ed came running out of the house with the baby and handed him to Leon and told him to take him to me. Fred and Ed put Joann in the back seat. They hooked up the horn to blast all the way to Morehead City, about 17 miles away. She was bleeding internally. They took off in our Mustang because it was a lot quicker than Ed's VW. Leon brought Shawn to me, and he and Jason were only a few months apart in age. They had a lot of fun playing. I kept food and coffee ready for Ed. He could only see her for five minutes every two hours. She made it through and got out of the hospital about a month later.

Things did not improve for us. They got worse. I sold Tupperware at parties in the evening. I would get the kitchen cleaned up from dinner and get Jason to bed before I left. Fred would have me call him from the party when I got there and when I headed home. He made out like he cared that I was driving at night on the curving roads. I found out later he had an affair with a female Marine. He would call her after I called him from the party, then she would leave when I called that I was on my way home. If I had known about it at the time, I would have left him then. As it was, about a year after my father died, we split up. He kept trying to get me back. I finally packed the car and Jason, and I left for Florida. We stayed with friends for a few months, then we moved to my sister's in Texas for about six months. Fred came there at Thanksgiving to talk to me. He swore the Marine Corps had been the cause of his bad temper, and he was being discharged in early December. So, Jason and I went to Fred's parent's home in Clearwater, Florida. Fred came there when he got out of the Corps. For a while, his behavior was better.

We bought a little house and moved in. He got a job right away at Honeywell Aerospace in Clearwater. Things went fairly well for a year. Then he got laid-off.

It was the recession of 1974. He signed up at a tech school so he could collect on his VA benefits. I've always been good with handling money, so I was in charge of the money. He started bringing people over after classes, and they would drink all afternoon and dirty up my living room and kitchen. I finally got a job of my own as a secretary at a Flight School. I left Jason with his dad and a friend for the day. When I came home, Jason nearly jumped in my arms and was very upset and crying. Fred made little of it. He told me he and his friend Bob took Jason fishing with them on a long pier. They let him run right off the end of the pier and drop into 60' of water. He could not swim. He was three years old. Fred said they watched him trying to get to the surface and finally went in after him. I was pissed!

The next day, Jason went to a nearby church-run daycare center. I told them Fred was not allowed to pick him up from daycare unless I said so. They were great. Jason and I started going to church there. Fred wouldn't go. He was brought up in the Lutheran church but had no belief in God anymore. I was raised Baptist. This was a Presbyterian Church. Jason was baptized there. We attended off and on for several years.

After 19 months of no work, Fred finally got another job. He came home after one week, threw his keys on the kitchen counter, and swore he was going to take off from work for another 19 months. Something inside me went cold. I told him if he did, he could pack his belongings now and go live with his buddies. That shocked the hell out of him. He didn't quit the job.

My brother, Ed, came back from California and talked to us about learning transcendental meditation. We did. It turned our lives around for the better. For two lovely years, we got along. Fred calmed down a lot and even quit smoking. Then, all of a sudden, he decided not to meditate at all and would create so much noise that I couldn't meditate either.

During this time, I almost lost most of my family in a car accident. My Aunt Etta was not a good driver, but no one else at Grandma's knew how to drive. She was a widow now, so she was the only driver for herself, Grandma, and Mama. My brother Gene had just moved to Orlando after retiring from the Marine Corps. He and his wife invited all the family except us to come over on a Sunday to see each other again and to have dinner. When they didn't show up, Gene called the Turnpike Authority and the highway patrol. They went back and forth with no real news until about 4 p.m. Then, a highway patrolman was seen in Gene's neighborhood, looking slowly around. My sister ran out and flagged him down. Before she could ask for his help, he asked her if she knew of any new neighbors from North Carolina. She almost went into shock. She then told him they were looking for "the Ladies," as we lovingly referred to them.

It turned out that Aunt Etta was driving and came up over a small hill. There was a car stopped in front of her waiting to make a turn. There was no traffic light. She went into the other lane to avoid a collision. Instead of avoiding one, she ran head-on into a just married couple and killed them. She and Grandma always sat in the front of the car. Their legs went through the firewall, causing great damage. Mama always sat in the back and was thrown back and forth during the wreck. None of them would wear a seatbelt.

The highway patrolman escorted the family to the hospital where they were being treated. Grandma and Aunt Etta were unconscious when they were brought in. Mama grabbed the patrolman's hand and told him to get her son. She gave the patrolman the address as best she could remember. She had inverted the numbers. The patrolman had a hard time finding Gene's place but wondered if Mama had accidentally given him the address backwards. That's how he found Gene, my sister, and so on. I wish we had known his name, so we could thank him for keeping on it until he found them. They called me at about 5 p.m. and told me what happened and to get over to Orlando. Fred, Jason, and I got in our van and took off for Orlando. We waited and waited together in the family room. Even the kids were subdued. About midnight to 1 a.m., two surgeons came in to speak to us. They had been working for 12 hours on Mama and Grandma; Aunt Etta was too unstable to do any surgery. It would have to wait. They put pins in each side of her knees and had her in traction. It was the best they could do. They had not treated the cuts and minor injuries as yet. We went to leave to get home, and my sister and brother told me to "do that thing that you do" to get Eddie here. He was in his van in or around the mountains in California. This was 1976. No cell phones or beepers.

When we got into the van, Fred asked, "What are they talking about to get Eddie?"

I told him that Ed and I have always been close, and I can contact him by sitting quietly and repeating his name in my mind.

"Oh bullshit, nobody can do that!" he said.

"Okay," I said. "You'll see."

I told him to please be quiet on the two-hour drive home. Jason was asleep. I started my thoughts going in Ed's direction. I just kept repeating in my mind, "Ed, emergency, call sis."

When we got home at nearly 3 a.m., I carried Jason to his bed. The phone was ringing when we walked in. I told Fred that it was Ed.

He said, "Bullshit, I'll answer the phone."

He did and turned white as a ghost. He handed me the phone. It was a collect call for me in my maiden name, from Ed.

When I answered, he said, "I heard you calling me sis, what's wrong?"

I filled him in, and he said he was leaving then to come home. It took him two weeks to get to us. The ladies went through 45 pints of blood in two days. I worked for a flight school and told everyone what happened. Instructors and students gave blood for them. Fred called the Marine Corps Auxiliary for help. Gene went to the Navy base in Orlando for help. The ladies had all the blood they needed, and then some. We drove to Orlando every evening after work to see them for about a month. It was grueling. When they began improving, we went every other day. This went on for over a year. That's how serious they were. The doctors had told us to plan on three funerals in that first week. The doctors didn't know my family. We are all very strong in body and mind. We are a mixture of Scottish, Irish, and Cherokee. Strong roots. That always comes in handy in an emergency.

During this time, Fred was actually pretty easy to get along with until he quit meditating. After about a year in the hospital, Mama went to a nursing home to live because she was a Paranoid Schizophrenic with homicidal tendencies. We all had children, and it was too dangerous to have her live with any of us. The nursing home was only about 15 minutes from Gene's home. He was able to check on her at odd times to keep the staff on their toes. Aunt Etta paid an ambulance to drive her home. She had refused any surgery on her legs. One was considerably shorter than the other, and she had to walk with a walker. The ambulance driver got her inside through a window. Etta had them hammer all the windows shut. No A/C, just a fan for ventilation. A lady from her church checked on her in the morning and evening. My sister was back in Texas. She did have a phone put in for her. One time, when Gene went to visit, he found the refrigerator no longer working. He bought her a new one, but she wouldn't accept it. She made a big fuss until he removed it. We would visit and bring food and drink. She especially loved lemonade.

She had a friend, a church member that would check on her in the morning and at night. One day when she checked on Aunt Etta, she found her on the floor, unconscious. She'd had a stroke and died a few hours later at the hospital.

45

Remember my high school friend, Dawn? She had married a Marine from Montana, and she had finally gotten pregnant. She was five months along when a neighbor came over with a phone message from Dawn's mother. She was in the base hospital and had lost the baby and wanted to see me. They knew about me and Leon. Fred said I couldn't use the car because he was going to the beach, and he wouldn't stay home and watch Jason. Leon was there and was supposed to go to the beach. He said he would stay and babysit, and I could use his car. Fred left anyway. Hell, Fred, why don't you just throw me at him! I got in touch with my sister, and she and her family were on vacation in Michigan. They would meet us on Friday night at a certain exit and then Jason and I would switch over to their van and go for a month's stay with them.

Well, all the "great plans of mice and men…"

Poor Leon didn't know what to do. We met a few times after that and just finally quit seeing each other. He got out of the Marine Corps and went to work as a civilian on base. I would call him and talk to him once in awhile.

Jason had his second birthday. I baked him his own little chocolate cake and one for the rest of us. He had a ball. He dug his hands right in and began eating it with lots of giggles and laughter. He had it smeared on his face and in his hair. I took him into the shower to get him cleaned up. We had bought him a little rocking chair of his own size, a red one. He loved it.

He also loved shrimp scampi and fresh bread. I would put him in his high chair to keep him from getting burned from the oven. We would talk and laugh. I would get my dough ready for baking. Then put it in to bake. It had a delicious smell when it was almost done. Jason would start flexing his little hands and wave them in the air.

Then he would say, "Ooh mama, bread, Mama, bread!"

I would cut off the first end of a loaf. I'd put butter and honey or jam on it. He would love it and want more. He was a really good eater.

I think he was trying to catch up. Hardly anyone could believe how much he could eat. When I was pregnant with him, I had hyperemesis and threw up several times daily until two weeks before he was born. I think that's why he was always so hungry. Years later when we had moved to St. Petersburg, Florida, there was a seafood house we liked to go to now and then.

When Jason was five years old, we went there. His dad had a dozen raw oysters and so did Jason. An elderly couple was sitting nearby and couldn't believe Jason ate a dozen oysters and wanted more. They paid for him to have as many as he wanted. He ate five dozen oysters and then a full meal with crab legs. These were not child size portions. He ate it all! Then fell asleep in the car on the way home. I think he was finally full.

He kept working, but his rotten behavior continued.

Our fifth anniversary, we went to The Colombia in Ybor City. It is an elegant restaurant that has been around for many, many years. You must have reservations. Fred stayed drunk all day and got into a minor car accident when he went to pick up our babysitter. We were late getting to his friend's house. Jim (from the Marine Corps) had set up hor's douvres and cocktails for us, but we were too late to partake. We went on to the Colombia. When we pulled up to valet parking, he got out and banged his fist on the headlight. While breaking the headlight, he cut his hand. We went in and were seated. He ordered another drink, and when appetizers came, he passed out and almost had his face land in the food. Jim and another friend, Buddy, carried him out and put him in Buddy's station wagon. Yeah, what a great celebration. I don't even remember our sixth or seventh anniversaries.

We had some friends, Sue, Garvin, and Sue's daughter, Misty. She was the same age as Jason, and the two played well together. They had a house wedding on July 4, 1976; the anniversary of our 200 years of freedom from England. There were tables out on the lawn, under a bunch of shady oak trees. Everyone brought dishes to share. They had no air conditioning, and the icing on their wedding cake began to slide. We had to insert a bunch of toothpicks to hold the cake in place. The wedding went off well. Everyone was happy for them.

In September, they had a party the Friday before Labor Day. Sue and I were off in a corner, talking.

She asked me, "What do you do when Fred beats you?"

I answered, "He's still alive and in one piece, isn't he? If he had ever hit me, he would be a ghost by now."

Turns out the bastard had begun beating her.

On Labor Day, we had a cook-out with family (Fred's Mom and Dad) and our friends. Sue, Garvin and Misty were included. Dad left to go see his mother, who was in a nursing home nearby. Fred and Jim left to go get more ice. While they were all gone, I was at the sink cutting up chicken. Mom came in with Jason in her arms.

Mom said, "Gloria, Garvin just kicked Jason in the stomach!"

I told her to take care of Jason, and I would take care of Garvin. I went outside and realized I still had a bloody butcher knife in my hand. I was highly pissed. Who did he think he was?

I asked him, "Garvin, did you kick Jason in the stomach?"

I just couldn't believe it. He said he did and to send Misty out and he would do the same to her.

I asked, "Why did you kick him?"

He said, "The kids were fighting, and I was tired of hearing it."

I told him, "Kids fight. Give them five minutes, and they'll be back playing again."

He wanted to argue about it. Really?! He was about 5'8" and probably over 200lbs. He also had a black belt in Karate. He drew back a fist to hit me, and I started laughing. I was so angry, all I could see was his face and movements, and it was all a bright red color. I stood my ground and got my knife ready to strike back.

I told him, "I'm not your wife, I'm not afraid of you, and I will hit back if you so much as touch me."

"Dammit," he said, "you're Celtic. You will never forgive or forget what I've done, will you?"

"No," I said. "I will never forgive you, and if my son is injured, he will go to the hospital, and you will be arrested. Now, I want you to gather up your family and go home. You are not welcome here ever again."

He, Sue, and Misty left. Unknown to me, they went to the store that Fred and Jim were at and apologized.

Fred's father had returned, and he was as angry as I was. Then Fred and Jim arrived from the store. Fred came in and grabbed me roughly by the arm, then escorted me to our room. He raised hell with me about sending them away.

Fred said "Garvin apologized, and I told him to come back to the party."

I screamed, "You did what?"

Fred asked, "What will you do if they come back?"

I said, "Call the police and have him arrested, like I should have done!"

Fred was on Garvin's side! He didn't even ask if our son was okay. We went back out to the living room, and he and his father got into it.

Dad said, "Remember when you boys were little and my cousin spanked you both? I beat the shit out of him for putting his hands on my kids. You didn't even ask how Jason is, but you sure are worried about your so-called friend. I don't know you anymore. This isn't what you were taught. We are leaving, and do not call me. I don't want to see you or talk to you for awhile."

It was six months before they spoke again.

I had told Fred that if that was the kind of people he wanted to be friends with, then I would help him pack his bags.

Then, Fred said, "I think I'll just kill myself."

I said, "Go right ahead, your life insurance is paid up. If that's really what you want to do, go for it." That shut him up.

The next day, Sue and Misty came pulling up. Garvin had beat her up very badly. She had all of her and Misty's belongings in her car. She had the only car. She came in crying and afraid Garvin might come by and see the car. I had her move it to the back yard.

Then, I saw to her many cuts and bruises. She refused calling the cops or going to the hospital. She said she was going to her daddy's in upstate Florida. I made her a bunch of sandwiches and snacks. She was afraid she would run out of gas. It was a payday week, and I handled the money, so I gave her the last $60 we had. They stayed a few hours, and we all took naps. Then she went on her way; I never heard from her again.

I finally talked Fred into staying away from Garvin. Just to prove what an awful person he was, about two years later, there was a story in the paper of how he shot and killed his Karate Master and went to prison. I don't know for how long. It was a bad ending for a former Marine who was studying to be a lawyer.

Fred had some good moments when he was meditating. I tried to get him to go back to it, but he wouldn't discuss it. He wouldn't discuss much of anything. We used to go out to dinner on Wednesday nights to give me a mid-week break from cooking. That was nice. I thought we might work out after all back then. We were closer, his temper almost disappeared, no more nightly ranting and raving. I enjoyed it, but then it went away with no explanation.

He began work again with a really good company. He installed equipment at banks. He had to start traveling out of town. In a way it was a relief, in other ways, it was worrisome. He would be gone overnight, or a few days, even a week.

He began to distance himself from me. We would be making love, and he would ask me, "When are you going to clean the toilet?"

Since I kept my house spotless on a daily basis, it threw me. What in the hell was he talking about? A few nights later, He wanted to know when I was going to buy another blanket. We had plenty of new blankets. What in the hell was he talking about? He would heap all kinds of guilt on me and cause me to cry and doubt myself. What I learned in later years was that he was cheating on me and felt he had to make me feel bad. I was so naïve still.

At Halloween, we went to a party that a bank teller he knew was giving. I had never met her until the party. She was about my age or younger, 25 years or so. She was very pretty and nice. But there was a definite undercurrent between her and Fred. I knew by the time we left there that she was who he was having an affair with. In looking back and knowing more than I knew then, he had several affairs during our marriage.

I used to ask friends, "How do you know it's time to get a divorce?"

I was always told it would be as clear to me as can be. On the day before our eighth anniversary, a Saturday, we and two other couples went out to eat at "Rough Riders" in Ybor City. It's a really great steakhouse. Everyone was partying except me. I had an out of body experience. As we were sitting there, my spirit rose up to the ceiling and was looking down at all of them.

I thought, What am I doing with all these people?

They were drunk, utterly stoned, and comparing notes on their sex lives. I realized I didn't want to be with them. It was not a great night. The next day was our actual anniversary.

Fred got up late. Jason was off to his friend's house, playing.

Fred came in and said, "I'm so glad you had a good time at dinner last night." He was being sarcastic.

I said, "You're right; I didn't have a very good time, and I want a divorce."

Well, you could have knocked him over with a feather. Eight years of very few gifts, or compliments. His best compliment was that one time he told me he guessed "he loved me as much as he was capable of loving." Is that a left-handed compliment? That's what he gave, if he gave one at all. I had had it. Too many years of too little.

He went to live with his friend Jim in Tampa. Jason and I stayed in the house. Jason had been having horrible stomach pains and was sent to the hospital by his school a number of times. He went to his doctor, and Fred went with us. Fred finally met Jason's doctor. A couple of weeks later, he had to go to his doctor again. They pulled me aside and told me it was emotional, and the best thing I could do for my son was divorce his father. After we split up, Jason's stomach pains went away and never returned. Emotions; they can nearly kill us if we don't do something about it.

I allowed Jason to see his father every other weekend. One weekend, I was invited by friends to go to Daytona Beach with them at their cost. I took Jason to Jim's place. Fred had just gotten up and was in a very foul mood.

He said he wasn't paying all my bills, just so I could go to Daytona. I told Jason he didn't have to stay, since Daddy was in such a bad mood, unless he wanted to. He wanted to stay. So, I went to leave. When I reached the screen door and had it open, Fred yelled what he yelled at me all the time.

"Why don't you just go fuck yourself!"

I nearly ripped the screen door off its hinges. I went back inside and jacked him up against the wall, with his feet off the floor. I was holding him up with my right hand. With my left hand I balled up a fist and drew it back and told him, "I don't have to listen to this anymore. We are apart now, and you don't tell me what to do or cuss at me, ever again. Do I make myself perfectly clear?"

He answered, "Yes!" and "I'm so sorry."

Then I let him down. He seemed sincere. Jason wanted to stay but was afraid of his father. Fred talked to him and got himself into a better mood. So, I let Jason stay. I had a lot of fun in Daytona. No sunburn, as it was February. When I came to pick Jason up on Sunday night, he had a good time with his dad and had his first swimming lessons. Fred had been a lifeguard when he was a teenager on Daytona

Beach. You see what I mean. Too little, too late. At least Jason was learning to swim.

Fred taught Jason how to salt water fish, and I taught him how to fresh water fish. We both taught him how to clean, filet, and skin the fish. He is now a grown man and still loves to go fishing. He always goes fishing when something serious is on his mind. He has always said that's where he does his best thinking.

It was with pure joy that I went through pregnancy and the birth of Jason. I took very good care of myself. No drinking alcohol or smoking weed. No medicines. I figured children had enough of a chance to come out with something wrong. I didn't want to add to it. He was the sweetest baby and little boy. He has always been sweet, except when his temper gets the best of him.

When Jason was 16 years old, he had a part-time job, and so he had money, a car, and a motorcycle. One night, he came home from work, and it was about 10 p.m. He got a shower and wanted to go back out. I said, "No."

He wanted to argue about it.

Finally, I said, "This conversation is over. If you want to continue to argue, go to your room."

He went to his room alright. He kicked the door off the hinges! I got up and went to his room. He was standing there staring at his door on the floor.

I asked, "You got paid today, didn't you?" He said he had. I said, "You better call all your friends and have them meet you here at 8:30 in the morning. Then, you're going to measure the door and go buy one at Home Depot and hang it, level it, paint it, and put a new door-knob on it. Do you understand?"

"Yes, ma'am, I do."

And so, his buddies showed up on time, and they spent the day putting his door on. When they finished, it was late afternoon, and I made them dinner.

When Jason was a toddler, he used to bring me a beautiful, pink hibiscus out of our yard. It only lasted one day, but it was a joyful way to start the day. After his nap in the afternoon, we would lay outside on the grass and look up at the clouds and the shapes they made. One time, Fred got home from work early and had to park across the street. We were laying in the driveway watching a blue rat snake that was hiding in a bush. We must have watched for an hour until it finally came out and writhed away. I don't know if that is what started his love of non-poisonous snakes or not, but over the years, he has had a few as pets. He currently has a baby Red Ball Python.

When I was a toddler, I used to scream and cry in fear over loud noises. A tractor coming down the road would scare the hell out of me. I would hide behind the old wooden rocker on the porch and scream and scream until Mama came out and picked me up in her arms. To this day, I don't like crowds or loud people. The funny thing about it is that I have a very loud voice. I once had an older woman at church tell me I was too loud. She was so quiet, she was difficult to hear.

I had a lot of fun with my son. At seven years of age, he began playing baseball. Then at eight, he added in soccer. On Saturdays, he had a game in both sports. I never missed a practice or a game. They were great fun. He played until he was about 12 years old, then we studied Korean military tai kwon do with a Korean war veteran. He was a great master and taught me it was okay for a woman to be strong and taught me not to be intimidated. After my husband, I really needed that.

At 34, catastrophe hit and pretty much ruined our lives. I became ill with a rare disease known as Guillain-Barre Syndrome. About 40,000 people a year in the United States become affected with it. Some live through it; some don't. Obviously, I lived through it, but it was a battle. It took four different doctors visits and two trips to the ER. The second time was the day of Jason's final exam for the first semester of ninth grade. I had been so sick since around

Christmastime, and no antibiotics would make me better. When I called paramedics the second time in 2 days, I was having a stroke.

Finally, I got to the hospital. A lady doctor met the gurney as we came in. It was very difficult to speak, but I managed to tell her that the doctors at their ER the previous night had done nothing for me. No x-rays or lab tests were done.

I told her, "I will die if you send me home."

I didn't know it at the time, but there was a lot of truth in that statement. I had no primary doctor because I was never sick. I lucked out and was assigned a really good doctor and after a couple of tries, an excellent male nurse named Tim.

They did a lot of tests and the final two tests would tell them if I had Guillain-Barre Syndrome, or Lou Gherig's Disease. I had a spinal tap and a CAT-scan. While I was in the CAT-scan I began praying to God. I told him how I wanted to live; I wanted to finish raising my son. Then I realized I was saying what I wanted. Then I prayed as my grandmother had taught me, to give my life to God, to give myself to his will, whatever it might be. I was shocked, but peace came over me, and I was told that I would live, but it would be difficult. That's all I needed to know. I shared my experience with my son.

And I told him, "if I die, turn closer to God, not away."

I told the doctors and my nurse that my son was very intelligent, and they were to listen to anything he had to say. My nurse drew us a diagram of the disease process and explained to us that it was a virus that had to run its course. Then, it would start to reverse itself. If I lived through all the secondary problems, I may be paralyzed for life.

Wow! What news, huh?

Jason and I talked, and I made sure he understood. He had to go live with his dad for the three-and-a-half months I was hospitalized. I was in a coma on a tracheostomy to breathe in less than 18 hours after sign in. I was paralyzed, completely, except for my eyelids, lips, and right forefinger. They tied a bell to my right fore-finger, so I could call my nurse. I was in and out of the coma. I had hallucinations. I also dealt with pneumonia, collapsed lungs, eye in-fection, bladder infections, crystals in my kidneys, and so on. They put me on a bed that sat at a 45-degree angle and rocked gently back and forth.

In my hallucinations, I was in a little cubby hole on a ship. The saline in my breathing treatments made it seem I was on the ocean. I would see my doctors or my nurse, but we were on the ship.

It was hard on me. I couldn't even move my head to the side when I vomited. I was ringing that bell as hard as I could. It was the night shift, and they really didn't take that good of care of me. Dur-ing the first week or so, I was in a private room, as they had no more room in ICU. Jason always came after school to see me. His dad would pick him up when he got off work. One day when Jason came, the drainage from my lungs was all over my face and dried in my hair. I had a private nurse who was reading a book and paying no attention to me. Jason went to the sink and got a clean wash cloth and wet it. He brought it back and began to clean me up. The nurse started yelling at him.

"What do you think you are doing?"

"Your job!" Jason replied, "My mother doesn't like to be dirty and all you're doing is reading a book."

He finished cleaning me up, then went to the hospital phone operator and asked her to page my doctor. She did. My doctor was in the hospital and came to my room. Jason told him what was going on and that he wanted the woman fired. She was. I never was ig-nored again.

My boss and some of the people from work would come to see me. When my boss came, he went up and down the ICU looking for me and couldn't find me. My nurse had to escort him to my bed. No one could believe how bad I looked. They didn't even recognize me.

We had three cats and one dog at the time. Jason would stop at the house when he got out of school and take care of them. A neighbor that loved cats took to putting water and food out for them on my porch. My ex-brother-in-law built a dog house for our dog. It was winter in Florida, but it can get pretty cold. When it dropped to the 20s neighbors came and got her and took her into their house and took care of her until the weather changed. She had a wool blanket in her doghouse, but at 20 degrees, she would have been very sick. I wish I could thank them again. They had moved by the time I got home.

When I moved into progressive care, I was told I'd never walk again.

I told them, "The hell you say! Oh, yes I will."

I made up my own exercise for that. I would sit in a wheelchair and use one or the other feet to pull myself forward, then the other foot. I would end up in the lobby, crying and in a lot of pain. A nurse would come get me and take me to my room and put me to bed and medicate me. It was very tough, but I walk now. I still can't run, but I can walk.

The lady who helped me was so very sweet. They moved away a little bit later to Brooksville. Her husband had built a ramp for me since we had steps to go up, and I couldn't do that as yet. When I came home, I was still wheelchair bound. He even hung a "pull rope" in case I tried to stand. She came every weekday and got me up and dressed, then she'd give me breakfast, and she'd drive me to Easter Seals for physical therapy. This was every day for about a year and a half. I worked hard and would do exercises at home that Jason would help me with. The county sent us a lady to clean and drive me to such places as the food stamp office. When we went there, I was in a wheelchair, and they kept asking the worker questions about me and my son that she couldn't answer.

I finally yelled at the woman, "I'm sitting right here, ask me. It's about me and my son. She comes to help us, but she doesn't really know us."

The worker said, "You have $130.00 in your bank account, you don't need food stamps."

Believe me, if I could have come out of that wheelchair, I think I would have done her harm, just for being an uncaring idiot.

I said, "Do I have to argue with you to get what I have paid into with my taxes since I was 14 years old? I obviously can't work. There's a letter there telling you so from two of my doctors. I can't walk or run; I can't go to the bathroom alone; I can't dress myself or use my hands as yet. Get your damned supervisor, and let her explain to me why I can't have food stamps for my son and I."

That did it.

She starting writing what she needed to, and I got emergency food stamps right then. Now why in the hell couldn't she just do that without all the hassle? I know there are government workers who work, and then there are the ones that should be paid commission only, as an incentive to get them to do their job. I really dislike people who are inept at their jobs.

I feel the hardest hit with this was my son. I'm an adult, I can handle tough things. But, he was only 14 years old. This was a lot pushed on him. Before he would leave for school, he would help me get up to the bedside commode and back to bed. When he got home each afternoon, he would come in my bedroom and see how I was doing and help me up to the bedside commode again. At first, he would stay home the rest of the day and night and didn't really get to see his friends unless they came over. His best friend's grandma lived two houses away and had a pond in her back yard where the kids loved to fish. It was a spring-fed pond with lots of bass and catfish in it. One day, I handed him my watch and said he needed to go fishing and take a break. He was very worried about leaving me alone. So, I told him to come back every 30 minutes to check on me. He did. When he came home for the evening about an hour later, he showed me about a 6 pound bass. He cleaned it and asked how to cook it. He did all the cooking. One of the ladies that came would clean up. We had the most delicious baked bass, mashed potatoes, and steamed yellow squash.

He used to put so much food on my plate it was unbelievable. I would fuss about it.

He said, "Doc said you have to eat plenty and put some weight back on, or he'll put you back into the hospital and continue feeding you through a feeding tube." Then he said, "Okay missy, you need to eat it all. I'll be checking on you."

Then, he went and got his dinner and sat on the edge of the bed to be sure I didn't feed it to our cats and dog.

It was all very difficult. At one time, I think he hated me because I took away his childhood too soon. But he's an adult now and finally realizes that I did not cause this. No one even knew what was wrong with me at first. We needed money coming in. My sister sent me enough each month to pay my small mortgage and to help with what food stamps didn't cover. My oldest brother paid my utility bills. I paid them both back in full when I got my first check for disability. And so it went. It was fairly normal, I guess, and then we had something happen that changed a lot of things.

This was seven years after Fred and I divorced. I had found out from Jason that when he stayed there while I was sick that he was treated badly. No one, not even Fred, had ever even once comforted him or reassured him that I would be okay. Instead, Fred got an illegal Power of Attorney. He waited until my nurse was off duty. The evening nurses didn't pay attention much. He held up my hand when I was momentarily out of the coma and made an X where my signature should be. A notary public that later became a second wife to Fred Sr. and a friend of theirs from the American Legion Hall that they belonged to were witnesses. Fred told Jason I was going to die, and he was going to sell the house; he needed the money. Now, if I had died, that house would have been for my son, not Fred. My oldest brother, Gene, lived in Orlando at the time. He came over every other day to see me. When Jason told him about it, my brother had a fit. He would take Jason out to dinner and visit with him when he came, then take him to Fred's. Jason asked his Uncle Gene what a "Power of Attorney" was.

Well, my brother knew Fred and wondered what he was up to. Instead of dropping Jason off at his dad's, he went inside with Jason to visit a little. He waited until Fred had a few black Russians and began to speak about things.

Gene asked, "So, what's this about a Power of Attorney?"

Fred said, "Well, the doctor said she's going to die most likely, and with Jason staying here, I need more money. So, if she dies, I'm selling the house, and keeping the money."

Gene just looked at him and told him, "If my sister dies, that house, car, etc., belongs to Jason, not you. If you do that, our sister might take you to court, but I will beat the hell out of you and send you to hell if need be. Do you understand me?"

Fred said he did.

About a week after I had come home, I was able to get into the wheelchair and come out to the living area. One day, Jason and I were watching TV together, and Fred came over. He sat down and then threw about a five-pound bag of papers at Jason, hitting him in the face, I started yelling at him, and he punched me in my left temple. The phone was near Jason, I yelled at him several times to call 911. I finally had to tell him to "snap out of it" and call 911 and "tell them his dad hit his mother who was paralyzed and in a wheelchair. Send the Sheriff's Office."

I had just begun learning how to transfer to a walker, and I tried like hell to get up on the walker. Fred saw that and headed for the door.

He told Jason, "Oh yeah, call the cops, tell them where I live, yeah you do that."

I told him, "We are." He left in his car. A few minutes later, a Pinellas County Sheriff's Deputy arrived. She was great! I was almost hysterical. She wanted to know what was going on, and Jason told her. While she was questioning us, I got a phone call from the bank. My bank. One of the tellers called me and asked if Fred could take money out of my account.

"Hell, no!"

He was there trying to clean out my bank account! He was cussing and swinging his cane around. She said he was jumping around with an angry red face. What should she do? I told her to call the police and have him arrested. Evidently, he left the bank, minus money, and came back to my house. We had given the deputy all the details by then, as well as the fact of what he had tried to pull with the house. And she was there when the bank called.

He came in laughing.

The deputy asked him, "What is so funny, mister? I don't find what you did to be funny at all. She won't let me arrest you because of your son, but you can't just go around hitting and trying to hurt people. She has something to tell you. I suggest you be quiet and listen."

The moment I began to speak, he started towards me, cussing fluently at me (I think I learned a few new cuss words) and angry, yelling at me. The deputy stepped between us and pulled her night stick and her .357. She ordered him to stop.

He told her, "You can't do anything to me; I'm a cripple."

The deputy told him "Well, she's paralyzed. She can't protect herself, so why are you doing this?"

He never answered. He did shut up long enough for me to tell him, "I won't keep your son from you, but you are to never, ever come on this property again, or I will shoot you dead. Jason can call you, go fishing with you, or stay the weekend, but it's up to him."

He stomped out of the house, and soon after the deputy left. Jason had gotten ice packs for both of our faces.

We wound up in court. My sister drove in from Houston to take us; I was still in the wheelchair. She, Jason, and I went together. I didn't know until we got there that Fred had filed for custody of

Jason. He was now 15 years old. The judge didn't like that Fred had done that. He even said to Fred, "Oh, I see. You wait until he's nearly grown, and then you want custody of him. Well, let's just see…"

He looked over at Jason and said, "Son, who do you want to live with?"

Jason stood up and told him, "I want to live with my mom! If you make me live with him, I'll run away, back to my mom's."

The judge told him to take it easy. He was staying at his mom's. Then he looked at the court and said, "I'm doing what should have been done" as he shredded the papers by hand "the first time I saw it. Now, let's look at your income. I see you and your wife make $100,000 per year, yet you have never increased the child support you pay. You will now pay $250.00 a month instead of $100.00."

I thought Fred was going to have a conniption. He turned red in the face, stomped his foot, and the judge reminded him what would happen if he didn't stop his behavior. The judge asked me if I had something to say. I did have something to say to him without being interrupted, and I wanted it recorded on the court record. He said, "carry on, ma'am," and told Fred to "keep his mouth shut and make no comments."

I told him again that if he ever put one foot on my property again, I promised him I would blow him apart with my shotgun. I told him, too, that someone may hit me once, but they sure as hell are not going to hit me again or threaten me or mine without dire consequences. It's how I was raised. Then I told him that I wouldn't keep Jason from him, but Jason would have to call and speak to him.

"Is that clear?" I asked.

The judge told him to answer me, clearly. He looked like he had murder in his eyes and said, "I understand."

Evidently, he didn't understand very well. About six months later, it was around Christmastime, and I sort of expected him to come around to see Jason. I was sitting at the table, and Jason was doing something in the garage, and guess who pulled up? Not just close but pulled up to the steps that led inside. I yelled to Jason that his dad was there and proceeded to the corner of the hall where a loaded, pump-action shotgun sat, waiting. I had to drag it back to my chair. It was still heavy to me. I put the barrel on the top of another chair and sat in the chair adjoining it. Jason ran through the living room, saw me, and asked me if I'd lost my mind.

I said, "No. You know that I told him what would happen. You better get out there and don't let him put even one foot on the ground, or I will blow it off."

Our front door had glass in it, and I could see exactly what he was doing. His foot was almost to the ground when Jason grabbed his foot and started pushing it upward, back into the van. I could hear his dad yelling at him, but Jason said, "No! She will blow it off. Let's go over to the school, like mom said."

I could hear Fred yelling, "Is she crazy?"

Jason said, "No, you just never knew when to quit pushing her. Now you've really done it. You are definitely on her shit list. Now, go."

There were no more problem with him showing up like that. They didn't speak for about six years. Then, one time when Jason was fishing at the family pier in Ft. DeSoto Park, he ran into Fred and they said hi. Another time, they saw each other and had a conversation. He let his dad know things were going good, and I was in college for nursing. They began to be in touch and salvaged their relationship. I didn't want to completely sever their relationship, as I believe a child should know both parents and develop their own opinion of that person.

Meantime, I was still in rehabilitation when Fred showed up at the house. Every day, I was getting stronger. I would even walk in the neighborhood on my walker and keep building up my strength. I once manually dug post holes in our backyard, mixed, and poured the cement for the holes and installed each of the fence posts, then strung the fence, all alone, in one afternoon, after cleaning the entire house and doing laundry. That night, I went dancing. That is how strong I used to be. No more. No matter how hard I tried, I never got my stamina back or the strength. Now, I have more strength; I beat the hell out of a guy that raped a woman I knew. Most of the men around the area where I live leave me alone. I've been told they are afraid of me. GOOD! Most of them are alcoholics, drug users, drug dealers, and prostitutes. I will help where I can, but hey, I'm very limited in what I can do. I try to give information to them that will help their situation. I'll even give free rides to the government offices that can help them. Some don't want the help; they just want to continue to be miserable. You can lead a horse to water, but you can't make it drink.

After about a year and a half, I was released by Easter Seals with a program I could continue to do at home on my own. I have done a lot of sports training in my years, and that helped. A lot of people never walk again because they can't stand the pain of rehabilitation. I had always wanted to be a nurse, and through vocational rehabilitation and my hard work, and Jason's understanding, I became a Registered Nurse. I passed my State Board Exam the first time around. I'm a lot smarter than most people think. I love it when I surprise them that way.

There was one problem: I couldn't seem to work for more than 6 months without something going wrong with me, either physically or mentally. I found my nerves were a bit shot and got worse as the years went on. I worked medical-surgical and wound care. My favorite that I worked in a bit longer was psychiatric, and I worked at a maximum-security men's prison with 600 inmates, and I was the only medical personnel. Passing medications, giving physicals to new prisoners, passing meds to at least 450 men a night. The only time a guard or officer was with me, was when I passed meds. They were usually young, inexperienced, and didn't pay attention.

Most of the other nurses hated me because I didn't feel that the men were garbage. They did not treat them with any respect or caring and would many times ignore their complaints, even when they were legitimate.

I was very busy one night. I had my regular duties; the exam waiting room was full, and they sent me 13 prisoners that had to have physicals and taken to their pods. I introduced myself to the "gentlemen."

I explained what I'd be doing. I explained I was swamped with work and to please cooperate with me so we could get through. I was not afraid of them. My karate master had taught me how to protect myself, not be intimidated, and how to fight back if necessary. Keep in mind a prison is so noisy on the inside, no one could hear you scream. I called the first guy. He came in and sat on the exam table.

At 7'3" and about 280 pound of muscle, a very large Black man was he. I go over again what I will be doing. Then I approached him and had to move in closer. I'm looking in his ears, nose, mouth, and all of a sudden, as I'm close enough to look in his mouth, he says to me, "I could rip yo' throat out."

That earned an instant survivor reaction from me. My left hand went for the family jewels, so to speak, and my right hand squeezing his throat. We were eyeball to eyeball and toe to toe. My nose was touching his nose, and I looked straight into his eyes. Gave a twist and squeeze to his Johnson and said, "I'll bet you could rip my throat out, but I bet I can rip yours out first."

And gave it another hard squeeze.

He said he would behave if I let go of him.

I said, "I'll let you go, but don't you ever try anything like that ever again. I am not afraid of anyone on this Earth, and you had better remember. I am not anyone's victim. Do you understand me?"

I also told him to check with the other inmates, and he'd find out I do everything by the book, but "Don't ever threaten me or play me, as it will go hard on you. I'm the only nurse around here that gives a damn if you live or die. I figure it's not my place to judge you. I don't know why you're here, and it's none of my business, and I keep it that way. If you are sick or hurt, I will do everything I can to help you. Even get you out to the hospital."

Then I finished his physical, sent him to his pod, and went onto the next one.

The next day, he saw me out on my rounds and said, "Hey nurse!"

I asked him, "How's your day going?"

He said, "I'm blessed, nurse, I'm blessed. How are you?"

"I am fine, thank you."

My first prisoner that needed medical help was an older Black man that hadn't been able to have a bowel movement in three weeks. No one would give him anything to help him. I examined him, and his belly was blown up huge, tight, and there were no bowel sounds. He could have ruptured and died. I sent him out to the hospital. I caught a bunch of crap from the captain.

I asked him, "If you were in the same position, wouldn't you want something done to help you?"

He thought about it a few minutes then admitted he would. When Mr. C came back from two weeks in the hospital, he was cleaned out; there was a new food chart of what he could and couldn't eat and regular daily medicine for him. He popped into the nurses doorway and told me the doctor said I was a good nurse, and that he would have broken open his intestinal tract in another few days, if not sooner. This small amount of mercy would save me at a later date.

We started getting in a lot of the young "gang-bangers." The older men that had been in gangs didn't like them. The young ones showed no respect to anyone. The older men and the younger ones would get into fights. The older men knew how to fight. The younger ones were used to guns, not hand to hand fighting, and so they were physically weaker than the older men who had fought with fists and knives. I had many "code reds" when these fights happened. It pissed me off. I was trying to pass my meds and had to stop and run with the very cumbersome and heavy med cart to the med room, unlock it, push it in, grab a 75 pound emergency bag, throw it over my shoulder, be sure the med cart was locked, then lock the door. Run, run, run to where I'd been told to the holding rooms on that unit. They would have the men separated. One man per holding cell.

Usually two officers would be in the holding area. I was to come in, assess their injuries, and treat or send out to the hospital. No one had to go to the hospital.

One time, this guy in his young 20s had been hit in the mouth, and it was barely bleeding. I went to clean it, and the guy tried to attack me. Before the officer could react, I did. I told the kid, "Do you want me to help you or not? I have never seen anyone fuss so much over a bloody lip."

Finally, he let me clean it off and put some antibiotic on it. You'd think he'd lost an arm or something the way he carried on. A few weeks later, I was passing meds. The guard with me was an airhead and just looking around but not paying attention to me. I saw someone was moving through the crowd quickly, coming towards me. I slammed the lock on the med cart and got ready to push it against someone. The punk got close to me and all of a sudden, a withered, black arm came out of the crowd and grabbed him around the neck, tight.

He said to the kid, "That be Nurse, boy! You don't mess with Nurse."

It was Mr. C!

He told that kid, "I done killed me five men, one more ain't gonna matter."

I said, "Thank you, Mr. C., you're a good man."

No one messed with me after that.

I dated a fair amount after the divorce. One of the men I dated was a local fireman. What a sweetheart! He was great with Jason and would take him on short motorcycle rides. He told me I scared him though because for a few weeks he was at my house every night that he wasn't on duty. It was short lived, but with fond memories.

I was engaged once. The closer it got to our wedding date, the more things I noticed about him. I had never been to his apartment in the year we'd been dating. He was tight with money. I met his mom and dad. Mom was nice, but his dad was a bit squirrely. He had met what was left of my family nearby. Jason didn't really like him. We had looked at a home to buy together, using my home as down payment. We had planned our wedding, talked to the preacher; I had my dress and shoes. One Saturday, Jason was at his dad's, so I thought I'd stop by Tracy's apartment. When I got there, I noticed someone was playing their stereo really loud. The closer I got, the more I could tell that it was coming from Tracy's apartment. I walked up the stairs and knocked on his door. Some guy in his BVD's opened the door. The apartment was full of young men in the nude or in their BVD's. Some were kissing on each other; one couple was on the couch, nude and making out. I nearly threw up! I ran down the stairs to leave, and Tracy had come to the door in his underwear and said, "Don't leave. Come back. We can work this out."

I yelled back at him that there was no way in hell we could work it out.

"Don't ever come near me again!"

With that, I left and went home. I called my friend Bambi, and we went to a country western bar called Joyland. She couldn't drink because it made her sick. I drank 15-plus salty dogs. My old boyfriend, the fireman named John happened to be in there. He saw me, and I told him what happened. He got me out on the dance floor to work some of the alcohol out of my system. He had never danced with me before. We danced a little while, then he took me back to my seat and told Bambi to take me home. I left and went home, passed out in my bed, and slept till noon the next day. That was the end of that.

Another one that got away was Jim. Jason has often said I should have married Jim. He was Iroquois, Potawatomi, and a little Hungarian. He was about 6'4" with black hair and brown eyes that turned black when someone (a man) was being rude in my presence. He lived on board a 44' wooden sloop named the Haze. He was retired from one of the vehicle manufacturers in Pontiac, Michigan. He had been raised in the streets of Detroit and had been a biker. When he was a baby, his mom would put him outside in a playpen, so she could work in the fields. One time when she came back, there were several rattlesnakes curled up on him and in his playpen. At first, they rattled their rattles, and then as if they realized she was his mother and he would be safe now, they slithered out the sides. This became a regular habit. No one was ever bitten. The snakes always left as soon as she showed up. I wonder what that means. We didn't see each other during the week because he worked, I worked, and I had Jason in baseball and soccer. There was a practice or game almost every evening. At Christmas, Jim came over and helped me wrap presents and put Jason's bike together for me. He was great with both of us. Such a gentleman. Sweet and kind. Though I doubt the men around him felt that way.

At one point, there was a girl from a psychiatric half-way house that would wait for Jim to come home from my house on the weekends. About 2 a.m. one morning, she scared the hell out of him. He came home from my house, got out of his van, and she popped up out of the shadows and told him that God had told her that he was for her and no one else. He told me about it. I told him he could take care of it, or I would.

One afternoon in February, I came down to the boats in the afternoon. We were sitting around with other friends drinking beer. Jim noticed I was cold and went down to my car to get my coat for me. While he was gone, we felt the boat move next to the dock. We thought Jim forgot something. It wasn't Jim. It was that girl. She was heavily chastised about coming aboard without asking permission.

That made the boat owner pretty angry. She sat down at the galley table across from me. She leaned towards me and said, "Jimmy is for me. God said so."

I told her she was crazy. I also told her, "Jim is mine, and that was according to him and me." Then I said, "Get the hell off the boat."

She took off running through the boat to the other side, and I told her, "Get off the boat or I will throw you off the boat."

The owner of the boat told her to get the hell off his boat and don't ever come on it again. She got off and left.

When Jim got back he said, "I see you had a little company."

We all said, "Yes, we did."

And the owner of the commercial boat we were on told Jim, "You need to talk to that woman and tell her don't be climbing on anyone's boat without permission. And tell her she was not welcome here."

Jim said he would take care of it. I was so angry at her and jealous. I am not a jealous person, but I sure was that day. One Sunday, it was only me and Jim on his boat. He told me he didn't only love me, but he was in love with me. He felt it was time for us to get married. I agreed. I knew it was right. He said he guessed he should get a job. I said okay. We started looking at getting married in a few months. I went home and told Jason. He was so happy that Jim was going to be his second daddy.

A couple of weeks later when I was on his boat, there were other people there that went up top when I got there. We were laying on the couch, and he said, "I love you, but I'm not in love with you."

I began to bawl my eyes out and headed for the door. I pulled the boat over to the dock and got myself out of there. Never heard from him for a year and a half. I did not date during this time because I was just too broken-hearted.

One Sunday afternoon, Jason was with his dad and there was a knock on the door. I couldn't imagine who it would be. It was Jim. He wanted to come in, and I let him come into the living room.

He said, "There is something I have to tell you. I'm going to prison tomorrow. When you would be home all week, I was sailing to Colombia to buy marijuana and cocaine and bring it back here for distribution. There were times when you, or you and Jason would be on the boat, and the hold was full. The DEA and local cops have been watching me a long time and finally caught all of us in Colombian waters. They let the old man off, and I got them to cut my first mate's time to one year. I have to serve 3 years at the nice prison in Alabama. It's where Martha Stewart went."

I told him, "I have no sympathy for you or your situation."

He said, "I didn't think you would."

He knew how I felt about drugs, most especially cocaine, or anything that was illegal. Then, he said he broke up with me because he knew it was only a matter of time before they caught him. If I was onboard the boat when the police searched it, I would have been arrested as well. It doesn't matter that I didn't know about the drugs onboard. I would have been just as guilty. I would have gone to jail and lost custody of Jason. I'm glad Jim thought of that. We stayed in touch while he served his time. He got out in a year and a half instead of 3 years. We wrote and made plans. I owned my own home, but he wanted to buy another home when he got out and get married. When he was due to arrive back in town, I asked him to come to dinner that Sunday at 5 p.m. He showed up at 8 p.m. I'm kind of peculiar about having people over for dinner, especially after they've been gone a long time. He was drunk and loud. I got really angry. He's the only man that could calm me down fairly easily.

I yelled at him, and he just put his arms around me and told me, "I know baby, I'm an idiot. I'm sorry, baby, I'm an asshole."

Then, I couldn't help it, I started laughing heartily. I got over being angry but realized we couldn't be together. He drank a lot and used cocaine. I couldn't have that around me or my son.

One night, I was having a dream, a nice one of puppies and kittens playing with each other, when darkness crowded in. All of the sudden,

I woke up because I couldn't breathe. I managed to get my eyes open, and it was my mama with her hands around my throat, making it burn, squeezing the life out of me.

Mama had been going out binge drinking since I was about eight years old. She'd be gone for about three weeks usually. We never knew who she was with or where she was. We didn't know if she was alive or dead. She'd come home, same clothes on, shit and piss on her. Daddy would ask where she'd been. She always had the same excuse. She'd say she had been "babysitting."

Another time, a Saturday, Ty's cousin Mike showed up, angry at Ty. They had gone to the Ocala National Forest to play "Combat" and practice for 'Nam. They used real guns and real ammunition. Ty had shot a small piece of Mike's ear off. We cleaned it up and bandaged it for him. Ty showed up and thought it was funny as hell. We used to say that Ty was a little crazy. He was a wild one. We never knew he had an actual girlfriend. He would drive around Jerry's, the local drive-in restaurant, with two Black girls in his car. This was the 60s and no one was ready to see that. Everyone would just say, "There goes that crazy Ty."

He told us she was a "good" girl and a virgin. Guys were still hung up on the virgin thing. When they returned from their honeymoon, he came to our house. He came up the stairs to our apartment bitching and griping about virgins.

He was yelling, "Virgins don't know shit."

I said, "Well, I guess you'll have to teach her."

My sister had been married, so she and Ty went to the drive-in movie to talk. They smoked cigars and drank a case of beer and Ty took off his wedding ring and threw it out the window. Never did find it. He had to hurry up and buy a new one before his wife saw it was gone. Not long after the marriage, he went to 'Nam and served as a company clerk. He came back and headed for our house. He was so angry. While he was away, his wife traded in the Mustang and bought a new, cheaper to run, Japanese car of some sort. WOW!

Then, my sister and her ex-husband got back together and re-married. I only had a three-day warning to find somewhere to live. My sister had a car, I didn't. She didn't offer to move me home or take me with them. I found a spot at a rooming house. I now had a serious boyfriend, Tony. I moved to the rooming house, and I got a waitressing job to support myself.

I did okay for a couple of months. Then, I got really sick. There were no phones at the rooming house. Men were not allowed to come inside, even a relative. I had no one except Tony and his family. When I was so sick, I managed to get across the street to where two elderly ladies lived. I explained I was very sick and needed to call my boyfriend's mother. They were kind enough to let me come in and use the phone. I called her, and she and her little girl were on their way. The ladies helped me cross the street back to the boarding house. She moved me to her house.

It took me several days to be able to return to work. I took over the front bedroom away from my boyfriend's room. It was no problem. He worked three part-time jobs. His main one was playing the organ in a very good rock band. I wasn't 21 years old yet, so I couldn't go see him. The restaurant I worked in at night was one block from where he performed. He would often come by and stop in for a snack. He was usually home in bed and asleep before I got home. His mom would drive me to work, and one of the girls I worked with gave me a ride home.

Sometimes on the weekend, we would go to Gainesville to see the funny car competition or drag racing. He had a new Kawasaki 500 motorcycle, and we often went on rides with other bikers to Daytona, have a lunch, and ride back. We had a lot of fun until his older brother, David, came home for a visit from the Army. He had been in North Korea for a year.

When David came home, the girl he had been engaged to (a virgin) broke up with him. She had found someone else and got married. One night, I came home from work and everyone was in bed except

David. He and I sat and talked, and he tried to get me sexually involved with him. I said no, and I went to bed. I guess he had fun the next day. He told his mom we'd had sex together and, of course, told Tony that. I denied it but still had to move out because of the friction it caused. School had started again, and I was finally a senior in high school. My typing teacher helped me get a part-time job at the local post office. It paid better than waitressing job. Tony started coming around, and we got back together. David was gone back to the Army. Good riddance!

I was making A's in school and doing well, then I started getting sick again. I moved twice to cheaper places to live and ended up with friends. I started crying at night and begging for Tony to come over when he got off work. I would cry for no reason. I started sleeping a lot. I know now that everything had caught up to me. I woke up one afternoon, and Daddy was standing by my bed with tears coming down his face. Lois, Tony's mother, was with him. We had no car or phone, so I don't know how she found him. Of course, we lived in a small town, so she may have gone to the police station for help. I went home to Daddy's. We went to the doctor first. It seemed a long time to see him. When I did, I had my daddy come in with me. I could barely hold my head up, I was so weak. The doctor wanted me to be hospitalized, but I knew what Chattahoochee looked like and I told him, "I'm not going. You'll have to rope and hog-tie me to get me there."

He told daddy, "If she has that much spunk left in her, take her home. I'm giving her a prescription for tranquilizers, and I don't want her under any pressure."

Daddy agreed, and we went home. Guess who was there to take care of me. Mama. Yeah, great idea.

I slept a lot at first, then I started eating a little. I only weighed 108 pounds. I was 5'10" tall. That was way too thin. I slept till at least 11 a.m. each day. One day, I came out of the bedroom into the kitchen just in time to see Mama coming in the back door, draining a beer out of a brown paper sack. I lost it big time. I didn't like that she was there to start with, and this just blew it. I started screaming at her that it was her fault I was like I was. All the drinking and strange men in the house when I was younger. Someone made an appointment for me to go to see a psychologist at the library. Mama went with me. Great. No privacy to talk. So, I said nothing. Finally, I told Daddy she needed to go, and he got hold of Aunt Etta to come get her.

I started going out for walks once I got a little stronger. I saw a friend of mine, Vicki, who was now married and had a little boy. She also had a horse and a pony. It was in the evening, and I got in the car with her to go pick up her husband from work. When they brought me home, Vicki asked Daddy's permission to pick me up in the morning after she took her husband to work, stay the day, ride horses, and feed me noontime dinner. Then she would bring me home to Daddy's when she picked her husband up from work. It was a lot of fun. The horseback riding was very soothing. We were having fun doing this every day. Then she and her husband started having some problems, so that was the end of that.

Juanita, the lady who ran the Jiffie Mart convenience store, told me she had someone she wanted me to meet. She told me to be at the store that afternoon. I was there. Oh, my gosh! I knew his name was Mack, and he was tall, blond, and a preacher's son. When he walked in, I think I fell in love! He was gorgeous! He was about 6'2", somewhat muscular with longish blond hair and big blue eyes. Friendly, a smile on his face, easy to get along with… I met his family that day. What a wonderful bunch of people! His dad was older like mine was. His mom was a large woman of Scottish Highlander descent as Daddy and I were. Not fat at all, just large. He had a little sister named Becky who was a romantic. Then, I took him over to meet Daddy. Daddy enjoyed him. He would talk with Daddy whereas Tony wouldn't. But Tony could be a bit shy. I had come home in April, and I was at Daddy's until sometime in July. Tony only came there twice. I think our relationship was going down hill.

In July, a strange car pulled up, and it was my oldest brother Gene and his new wife. They came in to visit, and Gene told me I was going back to North Carolina with them to finish school up there. I didn't know he had not talked to Daddy about it. I assumed Daddy knew. He was reading his paper after dinner while we put my stuff in the car, including my cat. I didn't get a chance to say goodbye to Mack. I called Tony, and he came to tell me goodbye and take the kittens I had. Unknown to me, I broke my Daddy's heart again, leaving him alone. I turned 19 years old while I was in North Carolina. Daddy sent me the only gift he was ever able to buy for me. It was a beautiful set of precious peridot birthstones set in 14k gold as earrings. I hardly ever wore them, as I was afraid of losing them. They meant a lot to me.

It took nearly a month before I heard from Tony. He was even late on the birthday. He never called. I lived near a Marine Corps base, so I started dating. I got engaged to one guy, Nicky. He was from Pennsylvania. He was making the Marine Corps a career. He was only 19 as well but was already a Sergeant. We had nice dinners out, and Gene liked him. One night, we went to the NCO Club and had a pretty good time. Nicky had already started changing. We got to my place, and he started telling me how lucky I was to be marrying him. He was talented, good looking, doing well in the Marine Corps, and so on. I'd heard it too many times and had him give me his hand, which I put my engagement ring in and told him to go marry himself. The next day, he kept calling, and I would not answer him. As far as I was concerned, that was it between us.

School was going great. I was taking more advanced secretarial and bookkeeping courses, so I could get a job after graduation and go to college. I wanted to be a registered nurse. That didn't come until many years later.

I loved the beach in the winter time, still do. I like the crashing waves and the wind blowing in my hair. One Sunday afternoon, my friend Dawn and I drove to nearby Atlantic Beach and were walking up and down the beach. The beach was deserted except for two young marines. We kept passing each other and then said hello. I met Fred. That was it. I thought I had been in love before, but I really hadn't. My friends didn't like him at all and kept trying to get me to break up with him. But he swept me off my feet. I had never had that happen. I fell deep in love with him. We conceived our son while on a long walk in a pine forest.

I don't know how to explain it to my son, but I need to. Even if it's here. I loved Fred with all my heart and soul. They say that if you survive the first year, then you're good to go. Don't believe it for a second. Our first little home was an 8'x38' travel trailer in a trailer park with other Marines and wives. I loved our little place. It was tiny, but it was ours. Fred used to say he could sit on the toilet, brush his teeth, and wash his feet at the same time. It was the truth.

One time, Fred's brother came to visit. Poor guy had to sleep in the second bedroom, which was a cubby hole of a bed with a sliding door at each end of the bed. No wonder he didn't stay long. Fred didn't like my southern cooking. Once he said he thought that "southern fried chicken" was all there was to southern cooking. Every damn day, I would clean our little place, maybe iron uniforms.

Let me tell you something about those damned uniforms! First, you wash them, then dry them after soaking them in undiluted starch, then roll them up while shaking them with water. Put them in the refrigerator and iron within a day or so. (You don't want them to mildew.) When you iron them, and I forgot to mention that from the washer you soak them in liquid starch and hang them on the clothesline to dry, you have to sprinkle them with water and then iron them before they dry. Always make your creases sharp. Use your 6" ruler to correctly space the creases in the shirts. Some of the bosses are assholes and walk around with a 6" ruler and check. Then you hang the shirt up and put the chevrons on it, correctly. Then, you do the pants. They are easier to iron and crease than the shirt. When you're finished, check all the clothing, especially around button holes for loose threads. Trim them. They are also known as "pennants."

Our neighbors were nice. We had couples from Kansas, Louisiana, Arizona, California, and us, from Florida. The landlady, Miss Salter was an older woman of large frame and some pretty big muscles. She was from "down east," an area of North Carolina that had only had a bridge to the mainland since the 50s. They had their own way of speaking and had a strange accent. If you weren't used to it, it could be difficult to understand. She had rules. We had to show her our wedding certificate at 7 a.m. our first morning in our new home. On the first of the month, she would show up at our trailers at dinnertime. If you were eating, she would excuse herself and sit with her back up against the door. If you're not laughing yet, you should be. Honest to God, she would sit there until we finished, and then she would knock on the door again. She had a good set up. She knew when everyone got paid. I doubt anyone ever got over on her. She had a very bad habit of going through our garbage. No, I'm not kidding. The guy from Louisiana got real tired of it. He liked his beer and she always complained to him about all of his beer bottles. To get even with her, he killed a large rattlesnake and put it on the top of the garbage in a position where it looked like it was going to strike. She pulled the top off the garbage can and saw that snake! They were all laughing. She grabbed her chest, turned very red, and nearly fell over. They had to call the EMTs from the fire department. She seemed okay but wasn't around for a few days. I guess she turned him in to his commanding officer or someone at the base. He got 30 days in the brig for Behavior Unbecoming a Marine, and Miss Salter evicted them. I thought the snake thing was mean.

We stayed there a couple of months, and then we moved to a bigger but cheaper place. Fred always told me if I had problems on board the base that I shouldn't handle it myself. I should look around for the most stripes or the most brass. Go to them for help. I went to the base for "cattle call." This was when only pregnant women were seen that day at the base. It was not for the timid. Or the shy.

About three months into our marriage, we went to the local fish house for dinner. The waitress was a girl named Gloria that I had gone to school with. She waited on us and was all smiley. I noticed she was wearing a beautiful pair of birthstone earrings, green peridot. They looked just like the ones Daddy gave me for my nineteenth birthday. I told her how pretty they were, and she thanked me and said they were a gift from an admirer. We had a nice dinner and went home. A couple of days later, I went in my drawer to find my earrings from my Daddy. Guess what. They were gone. The empty box was there. I thought our babysitter had stolen them. No one else had been in our home. She swore she didn't steal them, then she told her mom. Her mom weighed about 250 pound. A very tall and large woman. She called me over to the fence to talk to me.

One of our friends, "Shelley," was working on his car in the front yard. Fred was inside. I walked over to the fence to talk to her. When I got to the fence, she reached out and jerked all 120 pounds of me over the fence and commenced to beating on me. At first her daughter was yelling "get her mom, get her!"

Then Shelley jumped in. She was beating me really bad. It finally took five Marines to get her off of me. My husband was number six. That began to tell me something about him. He wouldn't take me to the hospital, so I drove myself. I needed a tetanus shot and some anti-biotics. I still thought the babysitter stole the earrings until years later when all of his cheating came to light after our divorce. Fred had a friend, Leon, who spent a lot of time with us. He was a very good friend. He took us all to see The Godfather movie and then pizza. That was very nice of him.

Friends starting coming around again after about a month. Leon came over a lot. Fred didn't pull his every evening routine of scream-ing, yelling, punching the refrigerator or the wall when Leon or anyone else was there. I wasn't used to such behavior. I thought he was an idiot. After the rape, my love went down to almost nonexistent. Leon treated me very well. He would often stay in our extra bedroom. He would come over on the weekends, and we would play cards a lot. Sometimes we would go to the beach. Fred wouldn't pay any attention to Jason, but Leon would. He called Jason his "little buddy."

My brother Gene was living with his girlfriend, so my brother Ed moved to North Carolina with his girlfriend and her son. Her little boy and Jason were only two months apart and liked playing with each other. They rented Gene's mobile home and 10 acres to live on. One day, Fred and Leon went over there to work on a car. About an hour later, Leon came back with the other baby.

He said, "Joann tried to kill herself. She shot herself in the stomach with a repeating rifle five times, then the gun jammed. Ed and Fred took her to the hospital in Morehead City, 17 miles away in the car. No time for an ambulance. She had internal bleeding. Fred said for you to take care of Shawn for now."

I got my neighbor to come over and take care of the boys. They were both about two years old at the time. Leon and I went to the hospital. Several hours later, she was in ICU. I kept the two little ones and tried to keep coffee on the stove and food ready for Ed. He could only see her for five minutes every two hours. This went on for a month. It was very tough on me. Leon was the only one that helped me. He was there most of the time. We would talk a lot and got to know each other. Turned out, he had a little sister he helped raise the first five years she was around. Then he got drafted. He would help me feed the babies and bathe them. He'd play with them. Fred didn't help at all, or even offer. But, he had to have sex every night no matter how tired I was. Leon and I grew closer, though nothing to be ashamed of. He didn't like how Fred treated me or the baby. We made a plan for me to leave Fred the weekend after the Fourth of July. I talked to my sister, and Jason and I were going to meet her and her family somewhere in Tennessee that Fred would drive us to. Once at my sister's, Jason and I would go on to Anaheim, California, to Leon's mother's home to stay and establish residency, then file for a divorce, and marry Leon.

The Fourth of July was on a Tuesday, and there wasn't much going on. On Wednesday, Ed came to my home with some bad news. Daddy had died in his sleep. We all had to get to Florida. I called Fred at work and Leon at work. Leon was the first one there. He wanted to bring me and Jason to Florida. I wouldn't let him. Leaving my husband and my father dying were too much for me. Leon and I had to put our plans on hold. I came home to Florida to bury my daddy. It nearly killed me. I loved my father very much and had great respect for him. If I cried very often, Fred got mad and told me to get over it.

I remembered that Daddy had always said he wanted to be buried in a plain pine coffin and no open casket.

He said, "If people can't come see me while I'm alive, they don't need to come see me when I'm dead."

We drove all night to get to Leesburg. We arrived at Daddy's apartment in the early morning. We found my mama, Grandma, and my aunt searching for a life insurance policy. I knew where Daddy kept it. What I didn't know was that I was the beneficiary. That made Mama angry. We left the baby with the downstairs neighbor and her baby. Our dads used to work together until her father retired. We took Mama with us to the insurance company where I turned in the insurance policy. From there, we went to Page-Theus Funeral Home where Daddy was. I picked out a pine wood coffin for him like he wanted and said no open casket visitation and paid for it. Then, we went over to Southern Monument Co. Mama had worked for them at one time answering the phone and doing some bookkeeping. I ordered a large granite stone with our family name on the top, and Daddy's info on it and Mama's info except her date of death. I didn't want to have to do this again. We picked up Jason and took Mama home. We stayed and visited a little bit, then drove to Indian Rocks Beach to my in-laws. I was so exhausted, I fell asleep on the couch. I called Fred's parents Mom and Dad. They said they were too young to be grandparents. We stayed there a day or two, and then we had to go back to Leesburg for the funeral. Jason stayed with my in-laws. We all gathered at Grandma's as usual. We didn't have enough pall bearers. Ed served as one and so did an old family friend who came to Grandma's. His name was Charles Chastain. I often wonder if he is still alive and living in Leesburg.

There were quite a few people there for Daddy's funeral. Mama and I had to compromise on open viewing. She got two days open viewing and then I requested that the casket be closed for the funeral. I didn't want to see my daddy dead. I wanted to remember how he was when he was alive. We had the funeral then went to the graveyard for a final send off. My brother Gene got there just as the graveyard service began. He had been gone on a Med Cruise, where the Marines go to practice war games. We had a difficult time getting word to the ship. I tried and failed. Joann was out of the hospital and was an Air Force brat, so about the third time I talked to someone at the base that couldn't help me, she took the phone away and took over. She finally got a chaplain that would help. My sister and her family had been in Michigan on vacation and, of course, were going to Tennessee to meet with me. We know how that turned out. After the funeral, my sister Loretta had us come and stay with them at her father-in-law's winter home in nearby Tavares. We stayed a few days with them. Gene stayed overnight but had to rejoin the ship. We returned to my in-laws for a few days and came home. The hardest part was cleaning out Daddy's apartment and learning Mama had sold the furniture to the landlord. There was a desk Daddy built for me for Christmas when I was 11 years old, but Mama had sold it, and I was not able to get it back. We had a long trip home. I was not yet 21.

When we got back, I let Leon know. He came to see me when Fred was at work. We talked a lot about the situation, and I had to tell him I just couldn't leave right then. It was all too much for me. My nerves couldn't handle it. We stayed in touch, but that was the end of it. Fred was fairly nice for a couple of weeks, then it went back to the screaming and yelling, jumping up and down in a rage, punching walls and the refrigerator. I have no idea what made him so angry. I had never known anyone so angry. I'm not including mother's anger in this, as she was mentally ill. That was the only other anger I'd seen.

Well, Fred was smart. He never hit me until many years later, and we were already divorced. Not long after this conversation, I left him and went to my sister's in Texas for about six months. On Thanksgiving weekend, Fred flew out, and we made up, and when he was discharged from the Marine Corps the following month, Jason and I met him at his parent's home in Indian Rocks Beach, Florida. We stayed with them until he found a job, and we bought our house. His temper never came out at his parents' but started again in our own home. Jason was a little over two years old at the time. He had a yard to play in, and he picked out a cat as his companion. The cat's name was Kippie, and he lived to 16-and-a-half years old.

Fred had a good job with Honeywell Aerospace for a year. Then they had a big layoff. It was the recession of 1974. He decided to use his VA benefits to go to electronic school, which he had already done in the Marine Corps, so he could collect his benefits for us to live on. He didn't want me to work, but I got a little tired of the burn marks in my furniture and tired of the beer cans everywhere. After morning classes, they all hung out at our house. I finally got out and landed a job as a secretary for a flight school. The first day I worked, I left Jason with Fred and a friend of his, Bob.

They took Jason fishing with them on a long pier. They let Jason right off the end of the pier and drop into 60' water. Jason was 3 years old and couldn't swim. He nearly drowned. Fred and Bob finally jumped in a saved him. Now that I was home he told me about it and was crying and hanging onto me. The next day he began daycare at a church. His dad did not babysit him again.

I said, "You did what?"

That Friday before Labor Day Garv and Susie gave a party. Susie and I sat in a corner talking. She asked me, "What do you do when Fred beats you?"

I answered, "He isn't stupid enough to beat me. I would hurt him or kill him for such a thing. You know you don't have to put up with that. Leave."

On Labor Day we had a cook-out with friends and Fred's parents. Fred and his friend Jim left to go get more ice. Fred's dad went to see his own mother in a nearby nursing home. I was in the kitchen cutting up chicken for the grill. Fred's mom came in carrying Jason (who was 5 years old at the time). She had a look of shock on her face and Jason was red in the face and short of breath. Mom said "Garu just kicked Jason in the stomach."

I said, "What?"

Mom repeated herself. I told her "to check Jason out and make sure he was okay." I went outside to talk to Garv. I couldn't believe he would do such a thing. I asked him, "Did you kick Jason in the stomach?"

He said, "Yes. Send Misty out here and I'll do it to her, too."

I asked him, "Why?"

He said, "I'm tired of hearing the kids fuss with each other."

I said, "Give them 5 minutes and they'll be friends again."

We started to argue. All I could see was a red tunnel with his face in the middle of it. I realized I still had the bloody butcher knife in my hand. I wielded it as a weapon. He drew back his fist to hit me. I started laughing. I said, "I'm not your wife. I'll hit back."

"Damn you," he said. "You're Celtic and won't forgive me or forget, will you?"

I said, "No."

I told him to "get his wife and child and leave. Do not ever come here again. You are not welcome."

So, he and Susie and Misty got into their car and left. There were 3 friends of Fred's on the porch through all of this. Not one of them lifted a hand or opened a mouth to help. I told them "they were all pieces of crap for not taking up for me and Jason." Then I went inside to check on Jason and Mom. Mom was still angry about what happened. Jason had got his breath back and was okay. Dad returned and we told him what happened. Boy! He was angry! He was very concerned about Jason and me. He said I did the right thing in having them leave. Fred and Jim returned from getting the ice. I started to tell Fred what happened. He grabbed me harshly by the arm and pulled me into our bedroom to talk. Turns out that Garv went to the store he and Jim were at and told Fred he was sorry. Fred didn't even ask if Jason was okay. He invited Garv to come back to the party!

He asked, "What will you do if they come back?"

I said, "Call the Sheriff's Deptartment and have him arrested."

We got into one hell of an argument, and I told him if that was the kind of people he wanted to associate with, then he needed to pack his bags and leave. Then Fred said, "Oh, I'm just going to kill myself."

He had been saying that a lot lately, and I was tired of hearing it.

I told him, "Why don't you do that. Your life insurance is paid up, so go ahead if that's really what you want to do."

Then I walked out of the bedroom and went back to preparing food. He came out and got into it with his father. His father was very angry with Fred and his attitude. He and Mom left. They didn't talk to Fred for about six months after that. The next day, Susie and Misty came over. She was beat up pretty bad. When they got home the day before, Garv blamed her for everything and beat the hell out of her. She had blackened eyes and a split lip, and busted up hands from trying to fight back. They were going to her father's home in North Florida. She had a full tank of gas, but no food or money. She and I made a bunch of sandwiches for her and Misty's trip. I gave her the last $60 I had. I knew that would get her there as long as the car didn't break down. They stayed a short time. She was afraid he might come there looking for her. I never heard from her again, but I know she didn't come back to him.

I forgot to mention that Garv was very muscular and stocky. He also had a black belt in karate. A couple of years later, it was in the paper that he shot and killed his karate master in an argument. He's still in prison for all I know. Good riddance to one more bastard.

Ed said, "I heard you calling me sis, what's going on?" I told him all that I knew. He said, "I'm leaving now. Be there as soon as I can."

He arrived two weeks later, but then he drove at only about 45 miles an hour, and Florida is a long way from California. Aunt Etta wouldn't let them do surgery when she became stable. Grandma had a stroke and a heart attack during her hospital stay. Mama did the best of all. She was in the hospital for about a year; Grandma was there the longest—about a year and a half. Then, Aunt Etta had an ambulance drive her to their home in Coleman, Florida. The driver's opened a window and put her in through the window! Then, per her instructions, they nailed all the windows shut. She stayed there alone until Grandma came home about six months later.

Mama couldn't live with any of us since she was a paranoid schizophrenic with homicidal tendencies. We all had children at home. It was just too dangerous after what she had done to me. She went into a nursing home for the next 15 years. But she was only about 20 minutes from Gene. He came by often and kept the staff on their toes. We visited her every month or so. However often we could. She passed away from congestive heart failure with my sister, Gene, and I at her bedside years later.

During this time, Fred and I had learned to use transcendental meditation to have a calmer, more peaceful life. It lasted a short time.

Fred was much calmer and easier to get along with during that peaceful interlude. Then, suddenly, he just quit. I'll never know why.

When Jason was in second grade he started having stomach pains. It was so bad he kept being rushed to All Children's Hospital in St. Petersburg. This went on for months. His doctors could find nothing wrong with him; neither could specialists at the hospital. One day, I had an important day at work, and Fred had to take Jason to his doctor for a check-up. I got a call to please bring Jason back in a week. When I did, they put Jason in an exam room with a nurse and asked to see me privately. Both doctors were very concerned. They said they had met his father, and it was their belief that Jason's problem was his father. They highly suggested I get a divorce, or Jason would soon be hospitalized with bleeding ulcers. Something to think about. Our eighth anniversary was coming up soon.

We celebrated our anniversary the day before, as our anniversary fell on Sunday that year. We got together with our usual set of friends and went to a really nice steak restaurant called Rough Riders in Ybor City. I just didn't feel happy or like celebrating. I don't know why. The problems with Jason's stomach was ongoing, and I couldn't help but listen to what his doctors had said. After about an hour of everyone drinking even more, a very strange thing happened to me. I had an out-of-body experience. All of a sudden, my spirit raised itself above all of us at the table to the ceiling, and I found myself looking down at all of us. I couldn't help but wonder why in the hell I was with these people. They were drunk and stoned and continued to drink, eat, and talk about their sex lives. Well, we finished dinner and went home. The next day was our anniversary.

Fred slept late. When he got up, Jason was off playing with his friends.

Fred said to me, "Well, I'm so glad you enjoyed our anniversary."

I said, "I didn't enjoy it, and you know what else? I want a divorce."

He couldn't have been more shocked if I had shot him. He just couldn't believe it! I told him he needed to pack up and leave. He did. He went to his friend Jim's.

I explained it to Jason and told him he would still see his daddy, often, but that Daddy and I had a lot of trouble getting along together and that sometimes that happens with people.

Jason said, "That's okay, Mommy. Daddy yells too much. He scares me."

Jason had no more stomach pains. Imagine that.

A few weeks after he left, I was invited to go to Daytona Beach with friends at their expense. I took Jason over to Jim's, so he could spend the week-end with his daddy. Boy, did Fred wake up on the wrong side of the bed! He was grouchy and wondered why he was paying all my bills and paying for a trip to Daytona.

I answered him, "You give me $100 for child support per month. That hardly pays my bills, much less a trip. My friends are paying for me to go with them."

He wanted to argue some more, and I finally told him if he was going to stay in such a bad mood, then Jason could come with me. I asked Jason if he wanted to stay or go with me.

He said, "If Daddy could by nicer, I'll stay. But if he's going to yell and be in a bad mood, I'll go with you mommy."

Fred settled down and said he was sorry, and it would be okay, so Jason was going to stay. As I went to leave, the second I closed the screen door, Fred screamed at me, "Why don't you go fuck yourself."

That did it. I nearly tore the door off the hinges getting back inside. I grabbed him by the shirtfront and jacked him up against the wall with his feet dangling.

I told him, "Don't talk to me like that anymore. I have listened to you speak to me like that for years. I thought I had to take it because we were married, well, I don't have to take it anymore. I won't take it anymore. Do it again, and I will punch your lights out, you hear me? I repeat, do you hear me?"

He said he did. His eyes were huge and staring at me. I don't think he thought I could do that.

Jason looked at his daddy and asked, "Do you still want me to stay?"

Fred said he did. Jason told him he had to stop being mean and stop yelling or he was leaving. Fred promised him he would behave. So, Jason stayed and got his first swimming lesson that weekend. I had a blast in Daytona Beach. When I came to pick Jason up on Sunday evening, Fred was much calmer and apologized for his rude behavior.

We were separated for 13 months. I felt if we couldn't work out our differences in that amount of time, it just wasn't going to happen. We got a divorce. We were better friends for a while. When we had been divorced seven years, we all had something happen that changed things.

Around Thanksgiving, I became ill with a cold, then the flu, throat infection, and ear infection. No antibiotics seemed to cure the infections. This went on through New Year's. Then I started having problems walking and swallowing. I went to several doctors. No one knew what was wrong. One evening, I went to get up off the couch and couldn't. Jason called 911 for me. Paramedics came and so did my neighbor, who worked at the hospital and was on call for x-rays. We went to Metropolitan General Hospital, just around the corner. There were twin interns on duty. One of them took care of me. He did no blood work or x-rays. They just wanted to know if I was on drugs or drinking too much. No to both. They sent me home. I went to my neighbors for the night. They were having midterm exams at Jason's school. He was in ninth grade and was going to a school that taught the arts. He was doing well. This really screwed it up.

The next day, I got home and stayed in bed. The next morning was Jason's final exam for midterm. I sensed something was seriously wrong with me. I sent Jason to school. After he left, I got out of bed by pulling up on a chair by the bed. When I let go, I fell and started having a stroke. The right side of my face was pulling, and I had a phone under my pillow. This was before cell phones. I dialed 911 and got the paramedics there. The ambulance came and took me to the same hospital. A woman doctor met the gurney. I grabbed her hand and got her to understand that I had been there and left untreated. I also told her I knew I would die if sent home. I begged her to please keep me and find out what was wrong. She promised she would.

The hospital was full, and I spent most of the day in the ER. They ruled out a double stroke. I was starting to feel paralyzed. I could feel it if someone touched me, but it was very painful. But I couldn't move anything on my own. They did blood work and x-rays. Then they told me I had either Guillain-Barre Syndrome or ALS (Lou Gherig's Disease). They were going to do a CAT-Scan and a spinal tap to determine which it was. There is no definitive test for either one. They have to rule out several problems before diagnosing. While in the CAT-Scan, I began to pray to God. I realized I was praying selfishly, asking for him to let me live, let me finish raising my son. Then I remembered how my grandmother taught me to pray. I apologized to God for being so selfish. Then I began to pray and gave myself to God, that his will be done. I actually got an answer that I would live, but it would be difficult. No kidding. They determined that I had Guillain-Barre Syndrome.

When Jason came to see me after school, my nurse explained to us the working of Guillain-Barre. It seems the synapses in the brain are made of a protein called myelin sheath. The disease eats up the myelin sheath, making the synapse shorter. It can't get its message across to the next synapse. It results in the paralyzation. It is a virus and has many secondary illnesses. If you can survive it, the Guillain-Barre runs its course, and you survive. Then rehabilitation starts. Other than being paralyzed, I was in so much pain, they put me into a medically-induced coma. I had pneumonia, collapsed lungs, and my kidneys shut down leaving, lots of crystals which later formed kidney stones. I also had a bladder infection and couldn't urinate or defecate on my own. The only things that still moved were my eyelids, lips, and right index finger, which they tied a bell to, so I could ring for help. I was on a tracheostomy to breathe and a feeding tube for nourishment. I had so many tubes down my throat that the area where the esophagus and the stomach came together was torn. It also left me with a swallowing problem. Every year, I have to have an EGD to dilate my esophagus. This still goes on now. I was put on a rotating bed that sat at a 45-degree angle and rocked me slowly back and forth. My doctors had no experience with this disease, but my nurse, Tim, had taken care of several cases of it. He knew what to do and advised my doctors what needed to be done. Thank God they listened to him. He was great with me and my son. So were the doctors. I told them that my son was very intelligent and to listen to what he had to say.

They had no beds open in ICU at first, so they put me in a private room with a private nurse. Jason came in after school every day. He came in one day, and I had mucus from the tracheostomy on my face, and it had dripped into my ears and in my hair. Jason went to the sink and got a clean wash cloth and wet it with cool water. He came back to the bed and began to clean me up.

The nurse asked him, "What do you think you're doing?"

He yelled at her, "Your job. My mom doesn't like to be dirty, and you let her get dirty, so you could read your book."

He finished cleaning me up and went to the phone operator and had her page my doctor. He came to the room and Jason told him what happened and the nurse was fired on the spot. Then they had room for me in ICU, and they moved me. Jason caught the flu and missed a few days. He had to change schools to one close to our home. He would walk home and check on our cats and dog. A neighbor helped take care of them and feed them. My ex-brother-in-law was kind enough to build a dog house for our dog since she had to stay outside. Jason would ride his bicycle to the hospital. The ladies in the office let him leave his bike with them, so it didn't get stolen. They always had a snack ready for him and would stall him from going to ICU if my doctor asked them to. One day, they stalled him quite a while, and then he went to see me. He told me that my doctor and my nurse were standing outside of ICU. Their faces were sad. Jason says he thought for sure I had died.

They told him, "Her heart stopped five times today. We don't know if she's going to make it or not."

Doc told him he'd called every hospital he knew of like Shand's, National Health Institute, Cedars of Sinai, and so on. They all said he was doing all there was to do. Then he told Jason it was between me and God. Jason told him about me praying during the CAT-Scan and my hearing a voice that said I would survive. He said that was all he needed to know. He knew it to be the truth. That was the worst. There were no more times of my heart stopping after that day.

Gene, a retired Marine, used to come after work in Orlando every other day to see me. Then he would take Jason to dinner and visit with him. Afterwards, he'd take Jason to Fred's and drop him off. One evening, they were at dinner and Jason asked, "Uncle Gene, what is a Power of Attorney?"

My brother said his ears picked up on that one.

He asked Jason, "Where did you hear that?"

Jason said, "It's something my dad got over my mom. He says she's not going to live, so he's going to sell the house and keep the money."

My brother said, "The hell he is! If she dies that house, car, everything is yours, not Fred's. They've been divorced for seven years."

That night, when he took Jason to Fred's, he stuck around to visit. He waited until Fred had a few Black Russians and became very talkative. Gene asked him about the Power of Attorney.

Fred said, "Yes, I have Power of Attorney over her. They think she'll die, and I need the money. I'm going to sell the house when she dies and keep the money."

Gene said, "You do that and our sister might see you in court, but I'll see you in hell. Do I make myself clear?"

Fred said he did.

My nurse, Tim, worked from 7 a.m. to 7 p.m. Then I never knew who would be my caregiver. One night, I swore I smelled death. I rang my bell, and my nurse came over. She could read lips just like Tim could. So, I told her I smelled death and asked her to pray with me.

She said, "There is no God. I won't pray with you. And you can't smell death."

I asked her to call my minister, and she wouldn't do it. He had put a message on my chart that they could call him anytime of day or night, and he would come. I was very upset. When Tim came in, he always checked on me before he changed into scrubs. He could see I was upset and in a lot of pain. I told him what happened. He took that nurse over to a corner and had a little talk with her. I didn't see her again.

The elderly man in the bed next to me was the grandfather of a coworker. The coworker would come see both of us. At about 10 a.m., the elderly man went into cardiac arrest and died. I knew I had smelled death. It just wasn't coming for me, yet.

Not long after that I went into progressive care. I started physical therapy every day after my nap in the afternoon. The first day in therapy, they tied four belts to me, and four people helped me get up on my feet and stay up. I walked to the end of the ramp and looked up to see Jason standing there with a big grin on his face.

"Way to go, Mom! I knew you could do it!"

I had been told that I would never walk again.

My response was, "The hell you say! I will walk again, you'll see."

Over the years, I'd had a lot of sports training in basketball, track, fencing, and Korean military tai kwon do. It was a good thing. I made up an exercise of my own to strengthen my legs. After dinner, I would stay in the wheelchair and put out one foot, set it down flat, and pull myself forward. Then I would repeat it on the other side. I did this for hours, and a nurse would come looking for me and usually find me in the lobby, crying from the pain, and bring me back to bed. It worked though. I was still in a wheelchair when I went home.

One of the couples from my church helped a lot when I got out. The husband built a ramp for me over our steps. The wife would come over every morning after Jason left for school, and she would take me to Easter Seals for continued therapy. I was there about a year and a half. Your United Way at work for you. They were terrific. She would bring me home and get lunch for me, then clean up and help me undress and get back into bed. I stayed in bed until Jason got home from school. He would stay with me and cook dinner.

One day when I'd been home about a week, Fred came by. He came in to visit, I thought. He was in a foul mood and threw a huge envelope of paperwork at Jason and hit him in the face, then he picked up a large piece of clay that I used for therapy to strengthen my hands and threw it at me, hitting me in the temple, which hurt. I had been learning how to transfer from the wheelchair to a walker. I tried to get on the walker to go after him. He took off for the door.

I yelled at Jason to call 911. Fred took off telling us to call the cops. He said it sarcastically. He left, Jason called 911, and a Pinellas County sheriff's deputy was there in about two minutes. She was really nice. Jason told her what happened, as I had started to have laryngeal spasms. She wanted to call paramedics, but I said "No. I just got out of the hospital. I'm not going back."

While she was there, the bank called me.

"Is your ex-husband allowed to take money out of your account?" a clerk asked me.

I told them no.

The clerk said he was there trying to clean out my bank account. She said he was jumping up and down, swinging his cane, and shouting obscenities. I told her what happened to us and that she should call the police. I guess she didn't call them because next thing you know, Fred pulled up.

Jason started shaking and crying and told the deputy, "That's my dad, that's my dad."

She told him not to worry; she would protect us. He came up the ramp and in the door, laughing.

She said, "I fail to see the humor in this."

He said, "Oh, she's just over-reacting."

The deputy said, "Oh really, you want to see me over-react?"

She told him I had something to say to him, and he needed to be quiet and listen. I opened my mouth to speak, and he started towards me, yelling. The deputy pulled out her night stick and a .357 pistol and told him to stop. He told her she couldn't do anything to him because he walked with a cane. She told him she could do anything she wanted with him. So, he stopped.

Then I told him, "I will not keep your son from you, but he will have to call you. You do not call here, and you do not come here. I will shoot you dead if you put one foot on my property again."

He left. About a month later, my sister came to visit from Texas and went to court with us. Fred had filed to get custody of Jason. The judge didn't like that. He turned to Jason and asked him how old he was. Jason was very respectful and told him he was 14. Then the judge asked, "Who do you want to live with?"

Jason replied, "My mom, and if you make me live with my dad, I will run away to my mom's."

The judge told him he could live where he wanted and tore up the paperwork. Then, he looked at the financials on both of us. I had no income. My sister paid my mortgage and sent me some money to help with other expenses. Gene paid my utilities for me. I paid them back when I got disability. Anyway, Fred and his wife's income was $100,000 per year. The judge saw Fred still paid only $100 a month for child support, and he hadn't paid any at all since I got sick. The judge got really angry about it. He ordered Fred to pay $250 a month.

Fred stomped his foot and turned red in the face. He did this a few times. The judge finally told him if he didn't stop, he'd put him in jail. I told the judge I had something to say to Fred, but I wanted it on court record. The judge told me to go ahead. I told Fred what I had before.

"If you come to my home, uninvited, and come onto my property, I will kill you. Someone may hit me once, but they will not hit me again. Do you understand me?"

Fred mumbled something, and the judge told him to speak clearly. "Do you understand?"

Fred finally answered, "Yes."

That was that, I thought. A few months later was Christmas. Jason didn't call his dad. One afternoon, Fred pulled up in his van. Jason was in the garage, so I yelled to him his dad was here and to go out there and don't let his dad step down on the grass, or I would shoot him. Meanwhile, I had taken the shotgun out of the corner and laid the barrel on top of a kitchen chair to help me hold it up. I sat in the chair behind it. When Jason opened the front door, I saw Fred starting to put his foot down towards the ground to get out of his van. I rifled down a bullet in the chamber and aimed. Jason got to him and pushed his foot back up into the van. He got his dad to go over to the school across the street.

His dad asked if I'd gone crazy.

Jason said, "No, you just never knew when to stop pushing her."

They went over to the school and visited, and his dad gave him his Christmas gifts. They did not speak or see each other for about five years. The good part is that years later, he and his dad settled their differences before his dad passed away about a week later.

My brother Ed and I were very close. The few times he was home when I was little are mostly happy memories. He was eight years older than me. He left home the first time when he was eight years old. He had either robbed the only jewelry store in town, or he broke into and robbed the National Guard Armory of guns and weapons. I can't remember which one he did at age eight and what he did at age 10. When he was home, he was my playmate. Our house was the only one on our side of a four-lane highway. I had no one to play with. Mama was usually too tired, and my sister Loretta was too mean to play with, and she had her own friends. I learned how to read and spell when I was four years old. Ed would play with the tea set with me. We'd smooth some of the dirt in the yard and play marbles or do math problems or write out a word my sister spelled instead of saying it. It was usually a dirty word. I would tell on her, so she quit spelling words in front of me.

We drove up to see Ed at the Dozier School for Boys in Marianna, Florida. I think it was Ed's birthday. Mama had made a nice picnic ham, potato salad, coleslaw, iced tea and a birthday cake. He was daddy's firstborn. He was born breach-birth, one leg first, natural. No C-sections were done yet when he was born in 1943. My poor mom. It tore her up, and she was told to never get pregnant again. But, then she had us girls by cesarean. Ed weighed over 10 pounds! My sister and I were 5 pounds, 1 ounce, and 5 pounds, 2 ounces. Loretta was born two years after Ed.

Anyway, when we went to see Ed, he and I got some food and sat at a picnic table under some oak trees. They were very pretty with the silvery-gray moss dancing in the breeze all along their limbs. The shade was nice and cool. It was only April, but it was warm. We were talking and Ed says to me, "Sissy? Do you see that small white house over there?" He indicated it with a nod of his head.

I looked and saw it.

"Yes, I said, I see it. Does someone live there, Bubba?"

He said, "No. That's where they take you if you're bad. They make you take your clothes off and then they make you lay on the table, and they strap you down so you can't move. Then they tell you what you did wrong and beat you with different things. Sometimes, they touch our private areas."

I was so young, I didn't know what "private areas" were. But I sensed the seriousness of it. Years later, they closed it down due to all the physical and sexual abuse charges. Some 20 or so years later they found two or three anonymous graveyards, mostly black boys but a few white ones as well, with no identification on the white crosses. I believe the remains of one child out of all of them were identified and sent home. What a hell to grow up in! But, the state of Florida put him there.

When Ed was released from them for good, he came home. He got a job working at night setting linotype for a local printer. Walking home one night, drinking a Pepsi, the local police stopped him and asked him what he was drinking. He poured out his Pepsi and said, "I'm drinking a Pepsi, but I guess you'll have to check it."

I think that got him a ride home for being a wise guy. Then, one Sunday, Mama made fried chicken. We always had fried chicken on Sunday. It was one of a few things that Mama could cook well. Everyone was quiet because we were busy eating our good dinner.

Mama said to Ed, "You don't like my chicken."

Ed said, "Yes, I do, Mama. It's the best fried chicken I've had in a long time. You make the best."

Mama said, "You are just saying that."

Mama took off her shoe and threw at Ed, hitting him in the face. All hell broke loose. We had no phone. The nearest phone was at the end of the next block, across the highway. The cops showed up and were putting handcuffs on Ed. They were taking my Bubba away, and he hadn't been home for very long. I didn't like it. I bit the cop on the hand and then on his leg. Ed had to get me to stop. Then off he went.

I didn't see him again until he was 18 years old and married. He was in and out of my life for about 25 years. The authorities always knew something was wrong with his brain, but they didn't know what. Many times, they misdiagnosed him. They finally got it right. He has Schizoaffective Disorder. It's sort of like being a paranoid schizophrenic and bi-polar. You don't know until you get up what kind of day it will be. There is medication for it, but Ed won't take it. It finally got so that I couldn't take care of him. I haven't seen or heard from him in 16 years.

Did I ever tell you about Grandma and Grandpa? Don't know a lot about Grandma except her mother died young, and since Rachel was the oldest, she raised her brothers and sisters and took care of her dad. Great-grandpa lived until I was five years old. He was one of the first pioneers in Lake Co., Florida. He had the first set of orange groves. The grove is still owned by a cousin in the family. Not much to tell about Grandma. She married at 14 years of age to Charles Augustus Thomas. I think he was 15 years of age when they married. Don't know what went wrong, but I was told he died when Mama was 15 years of age, which would have been 1930. A cousin later studied our genealogy and found that grandpa Charles died in Chattahoochee in 1943. His mother also died there at an earlier time. Chattahoochee was the State Hospital for the criminally insane. In its earlier days, it also took in alcoholics and drug addiction. Grandma and her three children, Etta, Mildred (Mama), and Charles, moved to Key West, Florida. She met an older gentleman there who was in charge of the Civil Defense. They all moved to a little town named Coleman. It is near Adamsville and Wildwood. They built a home that had a country store in the front. Many of the farmers around came to their store. You could get penny candy right on up to ordering a new tractor. When we went to visit, Grandpa would give us kids a ten-penny bag, and we could go into the store and fill it up. We also got to drink a Coca-Cola, which was a new thing to us. What a treat! Grandpa was grouchy a lot, but I realized later on it was due to the pain of rheumatoid arthritis and no way to treat it at the time. He had no wheelchair, and none of us could afford to buy one for him. He had to scoot from inside the living area out to the store and sit up on a stool to mind the store. We almost always went to Grandma's and Grandpa's on the holidays, and sometimes on Sundays. Grandma was a good cook. So was the Negro lady that worked part-time on Friday's in Grandma's house. She helped to clean and to cook for the family. I know Grandma sent her home with a lot of food and a little money for her work. They were both Baptist women and got along well. Grandpa died when I was 10 years old.

Aunt Etta would go over to help Grandma. Aunt Etta married Melvin Reuben Ward, a farmer. He raised registered Brahma bulls, hogs, and watermelons. He did rather well. He died when I was 12. He hadn't been my favorite uncle. He always smelled like alcohol and had a few days growth of beard that he would rub your face with. At the funeral, Aunt Etta was smiling. She got a hammer and a box of nails from Daddy and went to her house and nailed everything shut. Even left her furniture there, which people broke in and stole. She moved in with Grandma. Later on, Mama moved in with them. Grandma never let go of her kids.

A few years after Uncle Melvin passed on, Uncle Charlie passed on due to pneumonia from alcoholism. A few years after that my Aunt Ellen, his wife, was murdered. She lived in a small mobile home, alone. Neighbors noticed her lights were on day and night for three days. They checked her door which was locked. Her purse and cigarette case were on the kitchen table, but there was no answer to the door. They called her daughter, Charlene. She came and met the Sheriff's Department there. She unlocked the door and went in. She went running to her mother's room and got one hell of a shock. There was blood all over the small room with blood splattered even on the ceiling. Someone had cut her in half in her bed (she was a small woman) and put her in a garbage bag and discarded her body on the railroad tracks. The murder has never been solved.

Years from that, Grandma got "weary" of living and quit eating. Eventually she died from starvation. That left Mama in a nursing home and Aunt Etta alone at Grandma's. The refrigerator quit, so Gene took her another refrigerator and a lot of liquids to drink and made to eat food for her. She turned it all down, even the refrigerator. She was very stubborn and wouldn't accept anything that we brought to her. She died from a stroke and malnutrition. Mama lasted a number of years more, then passed away from congestive heart failure.

When Mama passed away, I had no tears. I think I had cried all my tears out. All I could think was the monster is dead. Jason was married at the time and his first daughter, Samantha, was about 10 months old. He and my mother had always had a close connection. He knew she had very little money. When he was growing up, he got a lot of presents from family. When he got a birthday or Christmas card, it usually had a couple of wrinkled up dollar bills for him. He acted like he won a million dollars. When Mama got to where she didn't remember me, she knew Jason. She didn't know his name, but she knew he was someone she loved very much. Mama would take his face in both her hands and tell him how much she loved him and kiss him. She never told me she loved me. She showed it in my earlier years, but I don't remember her telling it to me. One time, Gene and his wife, Jason, Mama, and I all went out for a barbeque dinner. Mama was on a walker and needed a little help in the ladies' room, so I went in to help her. As we were standing in front of the mirror, and Mama looked at my reflection and said, "Why, honey, you're almost pretty."

That was as close as I got to a compliment. But she always had them for Jason. I have harsh memories and good memories of Mama.

When Ed came home at the age of 13, he started spending more time in the swamp. He would fish and hunt. We ate lots of fish, turtle, rabbit, and squirrel when he was home. He would also pull up sunken row boats and fix them to take out into the swamp. One day, he took me at the age of five years old and my sister who was 11 years old. We took some of Daddy's lumber to use as oars. We had a lot of fun. It was summer, so we had good weather and lots of sunshine to play in. We went out into the deepest part of the swamp and made the mistake of running over a sleeping 18' alligator. It was not happy with us at all. It started knocking its tail on the bottom of the boat, indicating it was about to knock us out of the boat. Ed took off his shoes and socks and sat in the cone of the boat with his feet and hands dangling in the water and trying to make us go faster.

We ran the boat up on shore, and Ed picked me up and ran. My sister was in front of us. I remember Ed telling Loretta to run in a zig-zag formation. We made it to the crest of a stream that ran between our side yard and the swamp. The gator chased us to that point. We came into the house all of us screaming and me crying at the same time. Loretta and Ed both got spankings with a switch from Mama and later, a belt from Daddy for taking me out there to the swamp. I was never to be in the swamp, period.

A short time later, Daddy bought a new axe. He had just put a sharp edge on it and gone inside for some iced tea when Ed came running over from the swamp and grabbed the axe and took it with him. As he was running out of the side yard, he yelled to me that a really big gator was trying to knock two men out of their boat. Ed ran back over, waded in the water, and killed an 18' "grandpa of the swamp" to save the two men.

He got his picture and that of the gator in the local newspaper and got to keep all the teeth. Geez, they were huge! Daddy was mad because he had to re-sharpen the axe, but he was proud of Ed for saving those men.

Another gator story happened when we moved to the other side of town, and I made friends with Sally. They owned a small farm that had a lake on it. I went there one day to go swimming. I had never been there before. We went into the lake, and Sally says, "Oh! Look old Charlie is swimming with us."

I looked to the left side of me, and here was a large gator swimming right along with us, within a few feet. He showed no aggression to us and then broke off and swam away from us. Once we got back home, I told Daddy about it, and I was forbidden to swim there again.

A lot of things happened around our house when I was five years old and six years old. We used to have real hobos come to our back door looking for food. Mama always kept the door locked. When someone came to the door she would tell them they had to work for it. They always agreed.

Mama would tell them, "You see all those leaves over there? You see that rake? I need you to rake up the back yard and put it in a pile. Then, I'll feed you good."

She did too. When they finished, Mama would give them a pie pan full of beans, greens, and cornbread with a mayonnaise jar full of iced tea. For some of the men, that was enough. Some came back for seconds, and Mama would give it to them. When they got ready to leave, Mama would make sandwiches to take with them of leftover bacon or salt pork in biscuits left from breakfast and another jar of iced tea. They never tried to harm us. People were different then. To me, it was an adventure to have new people around and see how they acted.

Daddy used to hire an old black man sometimes to help him. He was a master carpenter in a small town. There were several people that hired Daddy to put in their wood floors, a specialty in those days. The old man would come home with Daddy at noon for dinner. They used to know how to work back then. They would start early in the morning, go home for dinner at noon, rest a few hours then go back to work about 3 p.m. and work until dark. Daddy would always invite him in to sit at our table, but the old man always said no.

"Somebody see me go in your house there will be trouble. I reckon I better stay out here."

He would settle down under a large oak tree, and I would bring him a plate of beans, greens, and cornbread, and the inevitable iced tea. When he finished, I'd take his plate in, and Mama would refill it. I'd eat my dinner then. When I got through, I would go out and get the plate for Mama and more tea for the old man. He would then settle down in the shade and take a nap. Mama and Daddy would lay down for a nap in their bed, and Mama would pull me up on her soft, large abdomen where I could hear her heartbeat. It soothed me to sleep, and a couple of hours later, Daddy and old man would go back to work. I never knew his name.

Living by the swamp was interesting. Sometimes late at night, I would wake up because I heard voices and car doors closing. One time, I got up the nerve to look out the window. If there was a full moon, I could make out the men and the cars. If it was dark out, you couldn't see much. One time, I guess Daddy heard me, and he came in to check on me. When he saw I was out of bed, he pulled me away from the window and told me to get in bed and stay there. He said these were bad men, but they wouldn't hurt us as long as we left them alone. We did.

We didn't have kindergarten back then, so I started first grade when I was six. I had been reading since the age of four. I could spell, knew my alphabet, and so on. It saved me in first grade. It was a confusing year. Mama and Daddy had a drinking friend named Whitey Snow. He had snow-white hair and big blue eyes like my daddy, but not the look of kindness I often saw in my daddy's eyes. My sister took off across the highway to go play. Mama and Daddy left to go to the grocery store, so they left me alone with Whitey. He was sitting at the table, drinking something. All of a sudden, he told me I was pretty, and he told me to take my clothes off. No one had ever talked to me about "good" and "bad" touching, but it just didn't seem right to me. I bolted out the door and ran across the highway, which I wasn't supposed to do, and over to my sister. I told her what happened, and she made sure he hadn't touched me, and I was okay. She said we would stay there until Mama and Daddy got home. When they did get home, my sister ran off and left me alone. It never occurred to me to ask for help from one of my friend's parents. Daddy was unloading the car, and I guess Mama was inside putting things away. I decided to cross the highway to go home.

I remember a car on the highway that stopped when it saw me trying to cross the four-lane highway, then they moved forward when I did. We couldn't seem to get the timing down right, and I ended up getting hit by the car. I lucked out once again. Sort of. I landed in a big patch of sand spurs and was knocked out at first. I woke up in an ambulance (our county had only one ambulance) with the siren going. I started crying, and I was laying across mama's lap. She was in the ambulance with me.

They did some x-rays and pulled a lot of sandspur thorns out of me. I got to go home as nothing was broken, no cuts. Who says God doesn't watch over little children and fools?

One day, we came home from school only to find Mama and a strange man putting our clothes in a strange car. Mama told us to get in the car. We found out we were going to Orlando. We stayed in a rental house this guy lived in. We figured out he and Mama must have been in love. I don't know if he was my sister's biological father or who he was. I just knew my brother Ed and my daddy were not with us. We stayed away for two weeks. While we were in Orlando, we went to see Gene's grandmother. Mama was married to his dad before mine. During an affair, she got pregnant with my sister. Ed and I were the only two kids of the same parents. When we came home, daddy was chopping wood out in front of the house. There was no argument. The man left, and that was that. We were home again. It was never spoken of again. A short time later, we went again. It seems we didn't stay very long that time. We came home again and were welcomed back by Daddy. It did not happen again. I'll never know what it was all about. My sister and I both barely passed our class that year because we were out of school so much. My sister passed with good grades, and so did I due to my reading and spelling.

The Methodist Church in Leesburg had a small chapel that seemed to be open all the time. I used to pray for my mama and in my innocence asked that God heal my mother. I guess it just wasn't in the cards. That's a hard one for a little kid to talk about. Then when the schizophrenia got so bad, I just thought life was hopeless. But, I kept on fighting. Always have. Always will be a survivor.

In my later years, I went to a club one night for a drink and some dancing. I was sitting and watching everyone dancing and talking to a girl sitting next to me. A guy sat down next to me. Then he asked me to dance. I said of course. He warned me that his left foot dragged a little, but he would do the best he could. Actually, he danced very well. We went back and sat down, and he offered to buy me a drink. I said okay. We started talking and continued into the wee hours. He seemed very nice, gentlemanly. We made a date for the next night, and I would pick him up as his car had something wrong with it. One the way home, I was feeling a bit happy. I'd had some fun and met a decent looking guy with a good job. He even had manners!

I picked him up the next evening, and we went out to the same club. We had a couple of drinks and danced quite a bit. Then, we sat and talked. He introduced me to one of his friends, Donny. Donny had to pick his girlfriend up at 11 p.m. from work on the beach. Then we'd all meet up at Allen's house for a couple of drinks, music, and just hanging out. I thought it sounded like fun. And Allen had been a complete gentleman. I felt I might be safe with him. When Donny left to pick up his girlfriend, we left to go to Allen's house. I had not been inside yet and didn't know he had a roommate. The roommate came out of his room and met me. He had two beautiful Pyrenees dogs that he took back into his bedroom and he locked his door and turned the stereo in his room up full blast. We sat and talked for about an hour. Donny and his girlfriend never showed up. All off a sudden, Allen stood up and came over to the couch I was sitting on. Turns out, it was a sleeper couch that he slept on. I stood up, and he pulled out the couch thereby blocking an easy exit to the door.

I said I had better be leaving and went to step over the end of the couch when he grabbed me, forcing me down on the couch. He owned a pizza store and had great upper body strength. He grabbed the crotch of my slacks and ripped them open. No matter how much I fought, he was stronger. He didn't hit me, he just managed to hold me down and rape me. When he finished, he rolled over and passed out. I grabbed my purse and ran out the door and went home. I kept thinking about calling the police and going to the hospital. I knew I wasn't physically hurt. Instead, all I could think of was all the questions that would come and witnesses to our drinking and dancing and leaving together. I know how the cops treat women who have been raped. They seem to want to blame the woman for "bringing it on herself." I did not ask to have sex or to be raped.

I nixed the idea of calling the police, got a shower, and went to sleep.

The entire next day, I cried and plotted revenge. I also chastised myself for being "won over" so easily. That evening, I got ready and went out. I went to the same club, and no one had seen him. He had talked about different clubs on the beaches that he liked to go to, so I decided to look for him; with my .38 Smith and Wesson in my pocket, and it was loaded with hollow points. Thank God in his wisdom. He did not let me find the bastard. I even sat in a stand of woods across from his house, hoping to catch him when he came in from work or the clubs. Never once did he show.

So, I ended up, on my own, in a psychiatric facility. I knew I was about to "lose it." There was a large older man who started following me around the unit, and it frightened me. I started screaming and running from him. They had to redirect him away from me and sedate me. I had my son take the gun out of the house and told him who to give it to. Not a good idea to continue to have a gun nearby with the state I was in. I stayed about a week and went home. I did get counseling for what happened. Life went on. I didn't go out to clubs anymore or drink anymore. A hard lesson learned. You need to be in control of yourself at all times. Anyone can act nice, but it doesn't mean they are. Looks can be so deceiving.

About three years later, I was invited to a Labor Day party in North Tampa. I never went to Tampa on my own. An old friend and I were invited to stay the whole weekend, but I didn't have a car at the time, so they drove to St. Petersburg to pick me up. We went to their home on Saturday morning. People started showing up. Bikers mostly with their women. We were having a great time.

On Sunday afternoon, one of the guys asked our host Big Bob about ordering some pizzas for lunch. His wife Rosie said there was a new pizza place nearby that was terrific. She went into the trash to find the place's phone number. The owner had just opened and was still writing his name and phone number on the pizza boxes. I saw the name on the box and nearly passed out. It was him! The one who raped me three years before!

Big Bob grabbed hold of me and asked what was wrong. I asked to wait and let me ask Rosie a few questions about him. What color was his hair? Brown. Most Italians have black or blond hair. Did he wear glasses or have facial hair? No. If she had to pick him out of a crowd, could she? How? She said he dragged his left foot a little bit when he walked.

I said, "that's the man who raped me three years ago in St. Petersburg and then disappeared."

Anyway, we didn't have pizza that day. I got myself calmed down and then went home on Monday. About a month or so later, on a Sunday afternoon, I get an anonymous phone call for "Gloria." I asked who was calling and a strange voice asked if I wanted a message from Big Bob.

I said yes. I couldn't imagine what it was about.

The voice said, "Remember how everyone wanted pizza? Well, Big Bob decided it should be minced seafood. Got it?"

I said I did and to thank Big Bob for me, and I owed him a big one if he ever wanted to collect. Once again, still a survivor.

The next year took a turn for the better. I have always been proud of my Scottish heritage on my father's side of the family. His mother was a Highlander Scot whose ancestors came from the Isle of Skye. I went to the Scottish Highlander Games in Dunedin, Florida and met some people in the Clan Donald, USA tent. They were very welcoming and helped me find where my ancestors came from on a map of Scotland. They had me come back for the parade and to have lunch with them and then dinner at a ceilagh or gathering at one of the members' homes. My grandmother was a MacCook who are one of the septs or families of Clan Donald of Sleat. Our tartan is made of beautiful deep red and dark forest green squares. Everyone was great, and I stayed in touch with a couple, Cathy and Bob, and also a woman I met there named Mary, who was a little bit younger than me. She belonged to Clan Ranald on the Isle of Skye. Over time, we all became good friends.

Mary and I hatched a plan to take a vacation to Scotland. We took a year to plan it and decided instead of two weeks, we would go for five weeks. It would give us a chance to see things. We rented a car. It turned out that it was half-price to rent a manual shift car than an automatic. Mary and I both knew how to drive a manual, and she was left handed. Since the driver sits on the right side, she did the driving. I was the navigator. I was a member of AAA and got several booklets and a map of Great Britain from them. I learned the best places to stay and some do's and don'ts, such as never asking someone for the chair their dog may be sitting in at the pub. No! Very bad idea unless you want the entire pub to be angry with you.

Anyway, when the time came, I had to have back surgery a couple of months before we went. My son was now married and his first child was on the way. I was 42 years old. We left at 8:30 p.m. on a Wednesday and arrived about 8:30 a.m. London time. We flew into Gatwick Airport. What was really cool was that the Victoria train station was inside the airport! What an easy way to get around. We took the train to a subway connection, then rode quite a ways on it. When we got to our destination, we only had to walk two blocks to get to where we were staying. There had been an ad in the Union Jack, a British paper that most true pubs carry. We had found an ad to stay in a private home (not a bed and breakfast) for 25 pound sterling each night. We had our own bathroom and shared a bed. We found out later that was cheap for London. We met the elderly couple and had some tea and a chat with them. Then I napped while Mary went out and about. She came back about 4 p.m. to get me. We got to see The Phantom of the Opera live with the original cast. I shall always treasure that.

While we were waiting to get a ticket, Mary went a street over to the Burger King. I gave her 20 pounds to get us some hamburgers and fries and drinks. She came back with two large fries, no ketchup as it was .12 pence for each little packet and a large coke to share. It took all but a few cents of the money. No, it doesn't taste quite like it does here. We ate that while in line. We finally had to get our tickets from a scalper. But we enjoyed it.

The next day, we went on a tour of the city on one of the double-decker buses. A tour of the Tower of London was fantastic. There were jewels and gowns from centuries ago. They were tiny people just a few hundred years ago. We found out that pubs and such close from about 2 p.m. until 5 p.m. We ate lunch at a hot dog stand that charged 6 pounds for a hot dog and 2 pounds for a soda. That was lunch. Later that evening we went to a nearby pub for dinner, as recommended. The food was great, and, of course, there was live Celtic music.

The following day, we checked out from where we were staying and headed for Heathrow Airport to pick up our rental car. We had read and heard about roundabouts but nothing prepared us for it. As we were leaving the airport, map in hand, we came to a round about to leave the airport. There were 12 choices. After our third time around, we just "winged it" and shot out in one direction. We ended up in Bath. This is where the Romans built the first public baths. We took a tour of the baths, and it was very interesting. They even invented heated water and heated living quarters. Where are these braniacs now? We went on from there and found ourselves in Wales.

Originally, we were only going to spend one day in Wales. You never hear anything about it. Well, we fell in love with Wales and used it as our base. We were on the main road into Cardiff, the capital. All the bed and breakfast places were hard to get to. It was a 90-degree turn off the main road (which was like a raceway with no signals), very dangerous. We turned down a couple of blocks and stopped at a stop sign that was across from a four-story bed and breakfast that looked like a lopsided birthday cake.

A young man came running up to the car and asked if we were lost.

We said we were, sort of. We told him we were looking for a bed and breakfast to stay in. He pointed to the one we sat in front of and said, "This is a good one, I'll go up and see if they have a vacancy."

They did! And they had a car park in back where they lock up your car, so it won't be stolen. We parked the car where we were shown to park, then came inside. We met the owner, Paul and his wife, Maggie. I got to be very good friends with them. We had a laugh when Paul and I first tried to have a conversation. Paul spoke very quickly, and I had to keep asking him to repeat himself.

Then he asked me, "What's the matter girl, don't you understand the English language?"

I replied, "I understand the English language, but I speak slow, Southern American."

Well, he had a good laugh over that. Paul was very tall and muscular. Easy to talk to. Maggie was short, a little plump, with beautiful red hair. We met their children. There was the oldest, Rob; then

18-year-old Martine; and 11-year-old Andrew. Andrew knew more about the Civil War in America than most people. He loved history. Rob was a chef and helped prepare a luncheon for the Queen and one of the princes. Martine stayed at home and helped her mom and dad run the B&B.

Mary and I went to St. Fagaans, the Welsh Folk Museum, several times. It was fantastic! They even had a small hut built as they did in the Bronze Age. They had a mill and a woodworker. Also, an ancient kitchen. There's just too much to remember. Everyone who worked there was very friendly. I found that the Welsh, especially in southern Wales, were very warm-hearted and kind and helpful. Just don't ask for directions. If you ask five different people how to get from point A to point B, you'll get five different answers, and none of them are correct.

One day, I was waiting at the bus station, and a lady heard me asking questions and realized I was American. She came over to me and told me how lucky they were during World War II to receive boxes from Americans. She said they received warm socks and caps during winter as well as food and vitamins the rest of the time. I knew from a friend's mother that they had no vitamins during the war. For pregnant women to get the vitamins, they needed their doctors wrote a prescription to their local pub for a free pint of Guinness beer each day, as it was full of vitamins and minerals. This lady affirmed it. She said her two boys still lived at home. As she was 82 she said; I don't think they were actual "boys." She asked if I had some gum or something she could take to them. I did, and I readily gave it to her. She was a gem and made sure I got onto to right bus, then waved me away with a big smile. God Bless her and her boys.

On our first trip to the folk museum, we met a young man who was working as a docent. His name was Dylan. He brought a lot of laughs to our visit. He had us meet him at a pub in downtown Cardiff. Cardiff is the capital of Wales, and so is the most populated. We met with him at the 4 Queens pub. They had beer and tables for talking and visiting with one another on the bottom floor. The top floor was live jazz. Pretty great. It was mostly college students and young professionals.

One evening, I was on my own and didn't know where to go. Maggie told me about a place the men went to. I went there only to have a man ask me what I charged. I was so dumb.

I asked, "Charge for what?"

He told me and then I noticed red lights around me. I frantically called the taxi station to send me a taxi. It took nearly 30 minutes for someone to come to my rescue. I got back to Maggie's, and boy, was I angry. She asked me what was wrong. I asked her if she knew she sent me to the red-light district. She blushed beetred and said she didn't. The men were horrified. They didn't realize that Maggie was as naïve as I was. I stayed in, and as the B&B had a small pub, I just stayed in there a while until bedtime. I didn't go out alone again.

While Wales was our base, we did go up to Blantyre, Scotland. It's about five miles from Glasgow. A friend of mine's Aunt Meg lived in Blantyre. When she came to visit them in Florida, none of them drove, so I would drive them shopping and to tourist attractions. I was always invited to come stay with her if I ever made it to Scotland. So, during the year of preparation for the trip, I wrote her and let her know that a friend and I would be coming over and asked could we come see her. She sent back an immediate invite. We stayed with her for a week. She was about a two-minute walk from the railway station, which she said was the easiest way to get around in Glasgow and in Edinbrough. We visited the museums there. And on the street corners were men in their Highland tartans playing the bagpipes for a little extra money. It was GREAT! You either love bagpipes or you hate them.

I happen to love them.

Our room was great. We had separate twin beds and a shower in our room. They had breakfast at 5:30 a.m. What a breakfast! We found out we were in a working man's B&B. The men came down on the train from northern Wales and from Scotland. They stayed there at night and got on the train to London in the morning to go to work. A lot of effort. Yes, they had families they went home to on Friday evening. Then, back again on Sunday. Great guys. Very nice, they talked about their families and work. When they came in about 5:00 p.m., Paul had pints of Guinness pulled up for them in their little pub. It held 11 people at a time. It was only for people who stayed there. We would all have a pint or two then go in to eat if you had set that up or go out somewhere to eat. Eating out is very expensive unless you eat Chinese food or Indian food. Hamburgers are not cheap. A large, hot breakfast was included with your room, but lunch and dinner was on you. Some B&B's will provide a dinner if you ask ahead of time. Our breakfast was two eggs, toast or fried bread, a whole tomato, sliced, a full can of pork and beans, and bacon. When you get used to eating all that, you don't get hungry for lunch until about 3 p.m. Dinner is at 5:00 p.m. or 5:30 p.m. So, we usually waited until dinner to eat again and saved some money.

In Edinborough, we were walking on a 45-degree angle on Princess St. when my right knee went out on me. That was tough. I just dealt with it until we got back to Wales to Maggie and Paul's. Maggie was great. She called her doctor, who was nearby and had me go for an exam. I hadn't broken anything, just twisted a bit. The doctor told me to wrap it and get a cane to walk on. Then she told me to go to the chemist and get some codeine pills for the pain. You need no prescription. The chemist is sort of like a doctor. You can go to them for a lot of your problems. You don't need a prescription for most medications. Even antibiotics.

We went up to the Highlands. We stopped in Inverness where Urquhart Castle exists on Loch Ness, where Nessie the Monster lives. We were met by a fellow in full Scottish regalia, playing his pipes for the tourists. My dad's mother's mother was an Urquhart. I didn't find any mutual relations. We went to the Isle of Skye to the Clan Donald,

USA center. The money for it was provided by the Clan Donald, USA members. I got to see documents with my ancestor's signature on it. We got to see Armadale Castle, which belongs to MacDonald of Sleat. All in all, it was a great day.

We saw beautiful waterfalls and natural gardens. We got to fight with sheep as to who owned the highway, if you can call a single lane dirt road a highway. They must be the dumbest animals on Earth. They just walk right out in front of you. At five miles per hour, it took us a while to get down the road away from the sheep. We saw thick, long-haired Scottish cattle. They looked like some huge beasties. We had lunch on Loch Lomond, cucumber sandwiches and lemon cakes. It's nothing like where I'm from. Very rural, almost desolate villages pop up here and there. No convenience stores and not very many petrol (gas) stations. We also visited the battlefields of Glen Coe (battle of the MacDonald's and the Campbells), and Bannockburn. The hair on the back of my neck stood up. We definitely were not alone. A bit of a wind came whipping past us at Glen Coe. At Bannockburn, I swear you could hear battle cries and the clank of swords. You could almost hear their death rattles as they lay dying.

We stopped during our travels for a night in a small village. It had one bed and breakfast in town, and it had room for us. We visited during the summer so we had "the gloaming" to see by at night. It didn't get dark until midnight, and the sun came back up at 4 a.m. After a dinner of sandwiches, we took off for the pub with a fellow from the B&B. Paul was from the Netherlands and was there to rock climb. He was a very nice fellow. We three walked to the pub. A nice bunch of people were in there. One lady came in with the most gorgeous German Shepard dog I've ever seen. He must have weighed 120 pounds. He had a beautiful coat and manners. She went over to a table and pulled out a seat and said, "Up laddie," and he hopped right up in the chair and sat pretty as you please with his paws barely touching the table. She took a large metal bowl from her purse and took it to the barman. He put it under a beer nozzle, and she took it back to the table for the dog. She set it on the table in front of him. She told him to wait. Then she went back to the barman and got her beer. She went back to the table and sat across from her dog to whom she said, "Drink up laddie." And they both did.

That dog did not get a single drop of beer on the table. He didn't look around or bother anyone. When the lady finished her beer, she wiped out the dog's dish and put it away in her purse, then returned her glass to the barman, and they left with the dog three steps behind his owner. One of the other patrons known as "Jimmy" was rather drunk but wanted to talk to us. He kept coming over to our table and asking questions about America. We had to clear up the belief that we do not live like they do on the television show Dynasty. It's amazing how many people we met that believed all Americans are rich.

A fellow came in that Mary had gone diving with on the River Clyde. The pub began to close about 11 p.m., so everyone could get up in time for mass the next morning. The guy that Mary knew was from New Zealand, so his nickname was "Kiwi." He suggested we all take a taxi to Ft. William, where there was a pub still open at a hotel. We shared a taxi, and he said he knew a lot of people and would introduce us to some of them at the pub. Well, after what seemed like an eternity, we arrived at the pub. Kiwi jumped out without paying his share of the taxi and went inside. We were left to pay for the taxi and when we got inside, he was at his own table and ignored us! So much for introducing us to others.

We sat at our own table and ordered drinks, then we talked about how rude he was and that someone should say something to him. Well, I decided I would be the one to speak to him. Against protests from Paul and Mary, I walked over to where Kiwi was sitting. I faced him, and he wouldn't acknowledge me at all. I spoke very loudly so others could hear me.

I asked him, "Is this how Kiwis treat people? If it is, then I want nothing to do with them. How could you cheat us on the taxi fare and lie to us about meeting some other people?"

He said nothing.

I told him, "You are a very rude person and I don't like you."

I was about to head back to my seat when a tall Englishman inserted himself into the conversation.

"Ah, that's enough of that woman. Why don't you shut your gob? No one wants to hear you."

I said, "Well you are not in this conversation, so you need to shut up and mind your own business."

Then I walked back to my seat. The Englishman did the same. They were sitting near us. We talked and went back to our own business. Things had calmed down, and the English group of eight and Kiwi and ourselves were the only people left in the pub. All of a sudden, the Englishman started insulting us again. I finally told him to buzz off.

He yelled out, "That's bloody typical."

I asked, "Bloody typical what? American, tourist, or female? What's bloody typical?"

I got up and started towards him; he got up and came towards me. We were yelling at each other, and he pulled back his arm to strike me. The next thing I knew, the barkeep was between us, and he had a large truncheon pulled to hit the Englishman and protect me.

He yelled at them, "You! English! Get out! You're banned! Nothing but trouble, you are. And you, Kiwi, out you go. You're banned too. You always cause trouble here."

They all got up with much bitching and griping. I thought, Well, hell, we're probably next.

Instead, here comes the barkeep with fresh drinks for each of us, on the house. Then he patted me on the back and said, "Don't fash yourself lassie. They're only English; they don't know any better, but you are welcome in me pub no matter what. And I like a woman with spunk."

We had our drinks and then walked over to the hotel to hear some live Celtic music. Then, we went back to the B&B. The next morning, we left and gave Paul a ride to the "3 Sisters," a combination of three mountains side by side. We went on from there. We drove around in the Highlands on several one lane roads. There are a few small villages. It's beautiful there. Waterfalls, farms with sheep all over, and some with the wild looking cattle that have thick, long hair with short horns. The were very docile, and they let us pet them. They don't eat much beef there. Also, right after we left Great Britain is when they had an epidemic of "Mad Cow Disease." The people in Wales and Scotland were very kind, helpful, friendly, and had lots of stories to tell. We found that the Scots didn't like the English very much and vice versa. Too much of a long history there.

I had a really bad asthma attack while in Scotland. I had to use a spray that you are supposed to rinse your mouth out with water. We were driving in the Highlands when this happened. We had both run out of water, and there were no places to get water. There were no convenience stores, restaurants, or petrol stations. The next day, we were in Oban. I went to the chemist and showed him my mouth. Sure enough, I had a yeast infection in my mouth. The chemist gave me some "swish and swallow," a tube of medicine with a little plastic spoon for the exact dosage. By the end of the tube, I was healed. After that, I made sure I carried two water bottles with me. We went back to Wales, and Mary took the car and went to Ireland. I was too tired. She was gone a few days and had an interesting story when she came back.

Mary is Catholic. Most of the Irish she met in Northern Ireland were Catholic. She had pulled up under a light in the village square and was going to sleep there. Two ladies came along after mass and saw her parked there with the American flag on the back window. They stopped and talked with her, and when they found out she had nowhere to stay, and that she was Catholic, they invited her home to one of the ladies' families. She said they fed her and had the neighbors in to visit and ask questions about America. She said there were cubicles built into the walls of the living room. She slept in one of them. The next day, she woke up, and everyone was gone to mass but left her a breakfast and a note thanking her for the night before. She ate and left them a thank you note for their hospitality. She left to come back to Wales. She also went back up to Meg's for another week. Meg lived across the street from the Pub, the only one in the village. It was still set up with a bar divided into two sections. One for the ladies and one for the gents. Yes, in this day and age! The fence around it is the original stone fence from over 1,000 years ago! We all had to duck when we went in and find a seat fast. It had a very low ceiling, and you could bump your head if you weren't careful. We would go over there after dinner and have a dram of single malt Scotch whiskey. It reminded us of another time, hundreds of years ago.

We got pictures of the queen when we were watching the changing of the guards at Buckingham Palace. I swear she looked right at me, so I could get a good shot of her. You really can't get the palace guards to talk to you. No matter what you do and say, they don't crack up at all.

Most of the time, the weather was misty with a soft rain. Thank goodness for folding umbrellas. I found out why the women carry such large purses and bags. They carry folding umbrellas, bottles of water, their shopping for the day, and who knows what else. I also noticed that the children go to school year-round with a few breaks during the year. We have year-round schools in the States, but not a lot of them near where I live.

Did I tell you about my Uncle David and Aunt Della? They were great. Uncle David was my daddy's brother. Their oldest brother, John, died in World War I in France. Uncle David served in World War I and came home undamaged. The middle son, Daniel was a chiropractor in Atlanta. I never met him. Daddy and Uncle Edwin served in the United States Marine Corps. They served the President of the United States inside the oval office as well as other Washington, D.C. areas. Daddy said they went to many balls at the embassy and served as dance partners for the daughters of Kings and Nobles the world over.

Daddy said, "I loved them all, but I wouldn't have married one of them."

One winter, his brother Edwin caught the measles but still had to stand guard in a blizzard at the Embassy. He caught pneumonia and died as a result. It broke my father's heart. Aunt Della and Uncle David went to meet the train when Daddy brought Edwin home. He was honorably discharged from the Marine Corps. Daddy had red hair, but Aunt Della said his hair had turned white by the time he got home. They buried Edwin in the family plot at Adamsville Cemetery in Sumter Co. That left Daddy, a master carpenter and master ship builder, and Uncle David, a farmer.

Aunt Della Colson Leigh was a very intelligent and educated woman. When Uncle David first asked her to marry him, she said when he built her a house, she would marry him. It took him four years to build the house out of cedar off his own land, by hand. When he needed a nail, he would whittle a small piece of wood to use as a nail. The house had two bedrooms and one bathroom. The house also had a tin roof. Boy, did it get hot in there in the summer, but it stayed warm and cozy in the winter, too. My uncle had made three fireplaces for heat. When he finished building and furnishing the house with some of his parents' and grandparents' furniture and some he built himself, he asked her again to marry him, and she did. My Aunt Della was also a strong- willed woman and spoke her mind. She could scare kids half to death. I know she was a member of the Daughters of the American Revolution. Not sure about Daughters of the Confederacy or Colonial Dames, but she had the right to all three as I do. Presidents John Adams and John Quincy Adams were cousins of hers (before her time, of course). Their son was named David Quincy Leigh and went by Quincy in the family until his father's passing. He was a great guy. Aunt Della boiled their clothes outside in a large, black iron pot. When Uncle David came in from the fields he had to wash outside on the back porch and put on clean clothes and shoes. The dirty clothes were left in a pile on the porch. There was a well pump, also known as a hand pump, on the back porch and a large enamel bowl to wash up in. She was ahead of her time. Liquid soap hadn't come on the market yet, but years before, my aunt put slivers of soap and a little water in an empty coffee can for my uncle to use to soap up. She also made her own soap.

Aunt Della canned a lot of vegetables and fruits. What they didn't grow, grew wild on their 160 acres. They had a huge fig tree that produced some delicious fruit. They had pecan trees, citrus, pears. We could hardly wait to get our Christmas tin from them. She made homemade fig cookies and fig newtons, wild plum cookies, peanut brittle, and pecan divinity. She had a grinder and would grind up roasted peanuts for peanut butter and bottled the peanut oil to cook with. She still cooked with and an old cast iron stove and did so until she died. Her son bought her an electric stove one year. She tried to cook on it and burned everything, then went back to the iron stove. She had a household garden just outside one side of the house. When the peanuts were green, she would boil them and can them for during the winter. They were good!

During the Great Depression, she worked as the only school teacher for the county. It was a one-room school for first through twelvth grade. She also drove the school bus. It gave them enough money to pay their property taxes—a very smart move. She also made use of old drapes. She sewed a lot and made some beautiful quilts, which won first place ribbons at the Florida State Fair each year. I helped her cut out pieces for the Dresden Plate pattern. Boy, was that difficult. She lost in competition that year because she accidentally left one pin in the quilt.

When I was a teenager, she once asked me if I had a bathrobe. I told her I didn't. Next thing I knew, they drove over to visit, and she had made a beautiful robe for me from some old drapes. It was great. She had kept many items of our hereditary information. She had letters from her family as well as the Leighs. She had letters from the American Revolution, Civil War, World War I, and World War II. When she and Uncle David had passed away, her son got rid of everything and sold the house and property to some people who raise butterflies.

The property had a natural spring on it, and when my daddy was young, the stage coach would water their horses there. The first person to be buried in the cemetery was a stage coach driver whose team ran away with him, and he was knocked to the ground and died.

David MacKendrick Leigh was my uncle. A kinder man I've never known other than my father. When their father, David Greenhill Leigh, died of heat stroke, the farm was left to those who still wanted to farm. Daddy got the house, which he sold, Edwin got the car. He and Daddy took off to see all 48 states that existed at the time. They succeeded. They joined the Marine Corps at Mare Island, California. They were both snipers and were sent to Washington, D.C. to serve. You know the rest of that story.

Many happy afternoons were spent on Uncle David and Aunt Della's porch swing. It was so beautiful and quiet. You couldn't hear any traffic, just the grasshoppers rubbing their legs and making their music. You could hear the wind swaying in the magnolia trees, and fruit falling to the ground from the citrus and other fruit trees, also the fresh pecans. If any of us kids wanted to go walking in the woods, we were required to take long, stout walking sticks with us. We were taught to pound the ground while we were walking due to an abundance of poisonous rattle snakes. He had a jar full of rattles off of snakes he had killed. We also had to watch out for quicksand. If you stepped in it, you could sink, and even drown. If you got into one you were to place your arms out to your sides and try to move very slowly to the side to get out, or someone's hand or a walking stick was extended to you and they'd pull you out.

Living in Destruction

When the farm first started, it was actually the Diamond L Ranch. They went out all over and gathered up short-horned wild cattle and drove them back to their land. I don't know how long that lasted. By the time, I arrived on the scene my grandparents had long ago passed away. Uncle David raised citrus and hogs. I found out at his funeral that he would hide $100 in a certain gate post as seed money for young farmers trying to get started, with the understanding they would put the money back in the fence post after harvest for someone else to use. What a truly kind and helpful gesture.

The nickname for Sumter Co. was "Hog County." The county was hit bad during the Swine Flu Epidemic of 1917. The only person in the family who got it was their one sister, Imogene. She was three months or three years old at the time. Daddy and Edwin helped two spinster sisters that came around on a buckboard and would pick them up early in the morning. They went around the county, house to house to see if they could help. They would bring food in a big cast iron pot and feed people that were still able to eat. They changed linens and took the dirty linens home to boil, like my Aunt Della did. Then they'd start out again the next day. A lot of people don't know that there was a worldwide epidemic of the Swine Flu. It killed one-third of Europe and was the end to the First World War. Everyone was so sick and dying from it on all sides. (This was also what was later known as Guillain-Barre Syndrome, which I had in 1984.) There was no one left to fight. I don't know about my father's life after the Marine Corps and before he married Mama. At the age of 40, he decided it was time to marry if he was going to have a family. He had known Mama since she was a kid. She was 14 years younger than daddy. They had a marriage of convenience. Mama was a divorcee with a young son who needed a daddy. Daddy needed a wife. He bought Mama a much-needed winter coat and married her. They both wanted to get away from their families and moved to Savannah Beach, Georgia, right after they wed. That was 1942. That is when their story began.

My Aunt Etta Dona Thomas Ward was my mama's older sister. She was tall and tiny. She always wore her red hair in a French twist. She married Melvin Reuben Ward a rancher and farmer in Sumter Co. He raised Registered Brahma cattle, some Angus cattle, hogs and watermelons. He owned about 1/3 of Sumter Co. at one time. My Aunt Etta was very quiet and calm. She bought me a new coat every school year. When I was 14 and in high school, she took me shopping for my first outfit for our Homecoming Game at the high school. We had the only high school in town. Homecoming was a big deal, and there was a dance afterwards at the Methodist Youth Center. It was well chaperoned and only cost 50 cents. Daddy gave me permission to go to both. My suit was a dark, olive green with tiny gold colored flowers on it. I wore it with a gold colored turtleneck blouse, matching shoes, and a purse, and Daddy bought me a corsage to wear on my lapel. I got several compliments from upper classmen. One of them, a senior, meant a lot to me. He is now the Mayor of Wildwood. Good for him. The colors of my suit went well with my dark auburn hair.

Aunt Etta was very quiet. She mostly spoke to the kids in the family and to Grandma, or other women in the family. She and Uncle Melvin had no children. When Mama divorced my oldest brother's father, she went away to Jacksonville, Florida (we think) for about six years. She left my brother in the care of Grandma and Grandpa and also Aunt Etta and Uncle Melvin. Melvin taught him how to farm and also how to hunt. The first time my brother Eugene went hunting, he got treed by a wild boar hog. He climbed up a tree and started yelling for help. Uncle Melvin said he and some other men came running. The wild hog was backing up and running forward, trying to climb up the tree after my brother. I hear the barbeque was really good. Eugene became very close to them all. In later years, when he was in the Marine Corps, he would be doing wartime somewhere, and he said he would hear Grandma tell him to get down. He would, and a second later, a bullet would zing past where his head had been. But then, we have that sixth sense in our family, and it has served us well.

I didn't care too much for Uncle Melvin. He had a rough way about him and usually stunk of whiskey. If Aunt Etta came over by herself, Daddy would always invite her in, give her a seat, and a glass of iced tea. This lady bought us some plastic drapes. Lord! I thought we were up there with the Rockefellers! She was always trying to help. She just didn't talk much. Now, if Uncle Melvin came with her, Daddy would carry chairs out and put them in the shade underneath the Oak Tree. He did not offer iced tea or anything else. One time after they left, I asked Daddy why he did that. He said Uncle Melvin belonged to a group of men that did really bad things to black people and to white people who had anything to do with blacks. This was around 1962. Times were getting ready to change, but not quick enough. It's now 2017, and it has only changed some. I guess all changes take time.

Uncle Melvin always said that when he retired he was going to drink himself to death. And he did. It didn't take him too long to do it either. At his funeral, Aunt Etta was smiling. I found out why. He used to beat her every night. After the funeral, we all went back to Grandma's to visit and reminisce the nicer side of Melvin. He left the property to his brother, not my aunt. He left her the house and the car and a small amount of property. She got very strange after Uncle Melvin died. She had my daddy go to her home and nail the windows and doors shut. She moved in with Grandma, who was also a widow by then. Of course, my mother was in and out of Grandma's as well. Grandma had a rocking chair in the corner of the living room, and Aunt Etta often stood between the back of the chair and the wall and would talk to herself quietly. She often acted as though she were pushing Melvin away from her and mumbling "no" to him. Aunt Etta was the only one of Mama's family that had a car. We hardly ever had one. The problem was that Aunt Etta was a horrible driver. She was color blind, and we used to say she would probably kill her, Mama, and Grandma one day. She almost did.

I was a grandmother now of three of the sweetest little girls you ever knew.

The first child was Samantha Marie. She was born during September after my trip to Scotland. Her mom had to have a cesarean section after several hours of labor. Samantha came out with her head pointed, also black and blue. Her dad (my son, Jason) rushed beside the nurse to an incubator. Samantha was crying, and Jason tenderly rubbed the side of her cheek and told her to please stay, that they had been waiting a long time for her to get here. She calmed down at the sound of her daddy's voice. She flourished and began to walk at about nine months of age.

The second and third children have a different mother. Jasmine Leigh was born four years later, with no problems. At 20 months, she got a little sister named Alaina Rae. They were all good babies. They are all grown now, and I feel very close to them. The oldest girl is married now and has a son. The middle one lives a couple of blocks from her dad in New York. The youngest one lives in a town near me. We don't get to see each other very much, but we stay in touch on the phone. We text a lot. They are all happy and healthy. I couldn't ask for more.

My father passed away when Jason was 11 months old. My mother passed away when Samantha was 10 months old. I wish they could have lived longer.

I started feeling really sick and didn't know why. I had trouble breathing, swollen ankles and legs. I went to one emergency room, and they sent me home with a blood hemoglobin of 7.2. Normal for women is 12 to 16. I was told to eat leafy, green vegetables for two weeks, and I would be fine. What a stupid doctor. I went home and had to sleep sitting up on the couch. At dawn the next morning, I was worse and slowly drove to a hospital I knew would take care of me. I drove across town to Bayfront Hospital in St. Petersburg. The emergency room parking was across the street from the ER. It was Memorial Day, and the parking lot was filling up. They had planted some new trees, and I had to hold on to one or another as I walked towards the street. They always had a guard in the ER, and he saw me having trouble getting to the road, so I could cross. He ran over and picked me up and carried me straight back into the midst of a very busy ER. I took my lab results with me and showed them to the doctor. They put me on a gurney and placed me beside the nurses' station so they could watch me. They did some blood work, a urinalysis, and chest x-ray. Then I laid there for quite a while. I was very groggy, and suddenly, the doctor said they had a room for me. The doctor was yelling for two interns that were placed on either side of me. The doctor yelled for a nurse to put a Foley catheter in me. He said I had congestive heart failure. I told him my mother died of that. He said there was no time to take me to the operating room. He said he was going to give me a large IV dose of Lasix to pull the extra fluids from my body. He said we could only wait a minute or two, if it didn't start coming off, then the interns would have to puncture my lungs and drain them.

The nurse got the catheter in; the doctor gave me 120 mg. of Lasix by IV, and about ten seconds later, the fluid started filling the catheter bag. The nurse had to run and grab a bath basin to empty it into. That is how fast it came out. Then she had to empty it a second time. My blood count was down to 5.8. They must have given me something to put me to sleep. I didn't know anything again until I woke up and saw a nurse hanging more blood for me. I was there for two weeks with no way to let Jason know. He was living in Tennessee. I went home and got better, but I was not real healthy. About a year later, in early May I was back in the hospital with congestive heart failure again. My legs and ankles were swollen and had ulcers on them. I had been there about two weeks when I got a phone call from Jason's ex-wife. Jason had fallen off of a waterfall, head first and was in a hospital in Nashville, she didn't know which one, only that he might live or die. I don't know how she found me. Then I got a call from his father. He didn't know any more than she did. Well, as any true mother, I pulled out my IV, undid the catheter, got dressed, and headed out the door. There were two nurses standing in the doorway. I told I couldn't take them both out, but I could take one of them out before I left, if they wanted to fight me.

"This is about my son. He's fallen off of a waterfall somewhere in Tennessee. He's in a hospital somewhere in Nashville. I need to get home where my phone numbers are. I need to get home."

They got out of my way and let me go. I had driven myself there, so I drove myself home. Don't remember driving home. I woke up enough to notice if it was light or dark inside the house. Though, I didn't know where I was. Three days later, the mailman realized my car was back so that meant I was back from the hospital, but I hadn't picked up my mail. The mailman went to a neighbor who had a spare key to my place. She and the mailman came in and found me on the floor, unconscious. They got me awake and something to eat. I told them about Jason. They helped me dial the phone, and my son answered! He had been in the hospital only two days in ICU. He had a head injury, his right knee cap was cracked, and the tibia and fibula of his right leg was broken in several places from the knee to the ankle. They wanted to do surgery to put in plates and screws, but he wouldn't let them. All the breaks were clean breaks so they put him in a walking cast. I had no money to go to him, so I called a lot. I think he understood. Would you believe it, his leg was completely healed in five weeks! We have strong bones and heal fast in my family. We are of Celtic blood.

I went to visit them for Christmas in Tennessee. We had a snowstorm two days before Christmas. I had to go to the hospital because I became very dizzy. I ended up on the floor and felt like I was going to fall off the floor. I had vertigo caused by Minieres Disease. There are three tiny bones in the deep inner ear. Sometimes movement, very loud music, or a change to cold weather will knock them out of place, and you become very dizzy. I went to a Blues Concert in Clearwater, Florida. No earplugs, brave and stupid me. The next morning when I woke up, I tried to get up and couldn't. My head was very heavy, as if iron were in my head. Also, I was very, very dizzy. Luckily, I kept a walker nearby because of back problems. I pulled the walker to me and managed to open it up. I managed to get to the bathroom using the walker. I kept a medicine on hand for these spells. It's over the counter, and I took two to start, and then one about every four hours. It's usually the next day before you get much relief. I don't go to concerts anymore.

I think Christy, Jason's girlfriend and mother of Jasmine and Alaina, thought I was faking it. They left after the ambulance carried me off at 10 miles an hour. (Remember, a snow storm was on going on December 23.) After the doctor in the ER released me, I had to take a taxi about 15 miles home. I think this was before cell phones. I had called their home several times with no answer. When I arrived at their home, no one was there. I had to stand out in the storm until they got home from Christmas shopping. Christy and I have had some good times together and a lot of bad ones. I don't like how she treated the girls when they were growing up. If my son or I had known they were being mistreated, we would have stopped it. I spent the next four or five days in bed. Little Jasmine was two years old then and would come in to see me and played by the bed, on the floor. Alaina was only 3 months old at the time. She mostly needed her mommy.

So, I stayed through the New Year, then flew home to St. Petersburg. I stayed home a couple of days then flew to my friend's wedding in Las Vegas. I flew home the next day. I was physically and emotionally ill. My depression and my diabetes got my attention for the next few years. My nerves were shot. They put me on Thorazine for awhile to keep me calm. I also lost my house that year. I was having trouble paying my mortgage, and no one could help me. I put it up for sale, but there were no takers. I finally sold it to one of those "We Buy Houses" investors. I packed up after 25 years in that house and left a lot of stuff behind. I moved with Gene's help to Jason's in Murfreesboro, Tennessee. I had a bedroom on the side of the house with the little ones. I didn't mind. I got to know Jazzy really well. What a little personality! So sweet. Even today, she and Alaina love me, and I love them very much, as well as my older granddaughter, Samantha. If she reads this, I hope she loves me as much as I love her. Let bygones be bygones. Call me. She stays in touch with her sisters, I think.

I liked Tennessee. Jason and I would sit out on the front porch and watch as a herd of deer gathered together for the night across the road from his house. I moved there on Halloween. That should have been an omen. I helped with the house and the children, and I gave them money from my disability check each month. In late January, at a Sunday dinner, Christy suddenly said, "Gloria, you have two weeks to be out of here."

WOW! REALLY? I think I went into shock. All my son did was call out her name.

I got up from dinner and went to my room. No one tried to talk to me. I cried, and I even begged God to take me, that my heart was broken. I cried myself to sleep. Yes, of course I awoke the next morning, and I went to my doctor about my diabetes. My report was good, but I was so broken hearted, I kept breaking down crying. Finally, the doctor asked me what was wrong, and I told her. She said she thought one of the girls in her office might know where I could go. The doctor talked to her and got the information of a Christian Homeless Shelter called "A Room at The Inn." The doctor called them and talked to the lady who ran it and got directions for me to find it. I drove there and met Mrs. Christine Huddleston, very much a Christian woman. We talked about why I had found myself a homeless woman. What my son and Christy did to me was very disrespectful. I have forgiven my son, but not Christy.

After our conversation, she told me to go get some clothes and come back the next day. I was still sleeping at Jason's, and I had two cats, Knucklehead (10 years old, a striped tiger cat), and Samantha's black and white cat named ZeeZee. I finally found a home for them on a farm. The next day, I went to a government housing complex called Spring Valley. They said it would be a couple of weeks before they would have an apartment for me. I gave them the number of the homeless shelter where they could reach me. I went back to Jason's and got my suitcase I had packed and kissed the girl's goodbye. Christy was smiling as I left.

I got to the shelter about 3:00 o'clock. I met everyone, and we went over the rules. About 6:00 p.m., some people from a church arrived with dinner. I believe it was three big buckets of KFC and the side orders. We even had plenty of sweet tea and dessert. The next night, it would be provided by another church. God Bless them all and the wonderful help they gave.

It was pretty calm around there. Two young sisters came to the shelter. By young, I mean 17 years old, and a 16 year old with a new baby. The baby was very sick. They took her to the hospital, and they sent her back to the shelter with a nasal suction bulb. That's it. I let them know I was an R.N. and to come to me if the baby got worse. In the middle of the night they were banging on my door. The baby couldn't breathe, and they couldn't suction enough mucus from her nose. I had to turn her upside down and actually put my hand in her throat and pull out the mucus with my hand, several times. She finally started breathing some. The older sister was sent to call paramedics. When they came, I told them what I did for the baby and asked them to please take the baby to Vanderbilt Hospital in Nashville. They did. I never heard what happened to them all. They all three stayed there. A couple of days after that, my apartment became available, and I left.

Someone from the shelter had a pick-up truck and helped my son get me moved in to my apartment. It was February 3, 1999. I was sitting out on my steps after I finished organizing everything. An elderly little black lady came over and introduced herself. Her name was Mrs. Lizzie McKnight. She lived in a nearby apartment. She asked if my couch was against the windows or the wall.

I answered, "The wall."

She said, "Good, because we sometimes have drive-by shootings, and if they can see your shadow they may shoot."

My door had no lock on it. This was Saturday, and they couldn't put it on until Monday. I pushed the couch against the door and slept on it so I would feel it move if anyone tried to come in, just like I did with Mama. All went well, and they put on a new dead-bolt lock on Monday. Due to Lizzie, I started meeting some of the nearby neighbors. A couple of years later, Lizzie died of pancreatic cancer. Another friend, "Little Mildred" died from Leukemia about the same time. I became very close to Mrs. Lizzeate Pendergrast. Her ex-husband lived in the apartment beneath me. There were four apartments on each side of the building. Lizzeate had three sisters and an ex-brother-in-law all lived there. They couldn't afford houses anymore. Her sister Frances had two grown sons living with her. One was very sick with Hepatitis C and AIDS. He died while I lived there. I went out with the other son to dinner one time. We went to a place about an hour's ride away to Bell Buckle Café. On Friday and Saturday night, they had a catfish dinner with French fries, coleslaw, and sweet tea for $6.95. They also had live Bluegrass music. It was great. On the way there, my date asked me if I'd ever heard the story of the woman and the snake. I said no.

He told me that one day, a woman was driving down the road when she came upon a snake in the road. She stopped and determined the snake was alive. So, she put him in a box and took him home. She took care of the snake until it was healed. One day she was petting it when it bit her! She asked the snake why it bit her.

Its answer was, "You knew I was a snake when you picked me up."

That gave me a chill down my back, and I never went out with him again. Turns out, he had been in prison for robbery and was a drug addict. He over-dosed on drugs and died a few years after I left Tennessee. His mother got cancer and died after both her "boys" had died.

Lizzeate had a sister who lived next door to her. Sally collected dolls. She had some really beautiful ones. Her ex-husband also lived in the complex. The older ladies still took care of their ex-husbands, cooking and cleaning for them. I never understood it. After I had left, Sally also got cancer and died. Everyone I knew up there has passed away at this point. Even a guy named Roger. His mother lived there, and so did he, in a separate apartment. I was going through menopause when I was in Tennessee. Poor men. I hated men at that point.

One time, I had several men come in from downtown that needed a physical before going to their assigned pods. I was swamped that evening. I had medications to pass, my exam room was full and then those guys came in. Wow! I had to get them processed first. I went into the room where they were and explained I would be doing physicals on each of them so they could go to their pods.

I only worked there a few months or so. Too much for one person to do.

I always talked all this over with Lizzeate. Thank goodness she was a good friend. I went over to her apartment on a Saturday, and her oldest granddaughter who was 19 years old came over with her boyfriend. Turns out, he had been beating her up. I couldn't believe what happened next. Lizzeate was 70 years old, but she launched herself across the coffee table and belted him a couple good ones. He left, and we talked her granddaughter into staying with her grandma. She and I went to where she was living and picked up her belongings and brought her back to her grandma's house to stay. Lizzeate didn't take any crap from anyone. Neither do I.

During this period of time, my son's girlfriend left him with no notice and took the girls. They were two years old and about nine months. We missed some of their growing up. Then, my son came over to stay with me a few weeks before heading home to Florida. He and his father had become friends again, and he was going to live with his dad and his family until he could get a job and save up for his own place. During that time, I'm happy to say my son and his dad got along well and made their peace with each other. About a week after Jason moved out, his father died in his sleep, peacefully with his cat at his side. It was a shock, even to me. He was 53 and had Rheumatoid Arthritis for a number of years. It really took a toll on him.

I had started working for the State of Tennessee at their State Mental Hospital. I liked that job. I did well after a hard start. I found out that the blacks (especially the women) were very much against white women in the workplace. I had some problems at first. I didn't realize it, but I was the only white person on my shift. And I was the charge nurse. Wow! They didn't like that. Anyway, I changed the section I worked in and continued to do well. My co-nurse was also an RN. We took turns being charge or medications nurse. We could do that being RNs. She had problems in the past with discrimination. Like her, I had joined the Union. She was provided a lawyer to help her keep her job. Reverse discrimination isn't a nice thing either. I had been there for six months and doing well, with good pay and great benefits when my son called me one night and begged me to please come home to Florida. Now, after getting a really good job. It figured. But I went home. I won't leave again.

I hired a couple of my neighbors to pack and load a diesel rental truck. Pulled my car up on the dolly and secured it and Bought a large carrier for my kitty "Gizzy." Away we went one early morning after working the night before. Don't do that. I made it to Chattanooga and woke up with loud, truckers blowing their horns and blocking me in. I had fallen asleep! I waved them off and exited to the first hotel I saw. Got something to eat and slept for about seven hours! Guess I was tired. Then Gizzy and I loaded up and hit the road again. I don't know where those truckers are now, but I hope the Lord watches over them and keeps them safe in their travels.

We drove straight through from Chattanooga, Tennessee, to Clearwater, Florida. We arrived at 7:30 a.m. on a Saturday morning. I stopped and called Jason, but they were still asleep. I already had an apartment picked out. I went there, but no one was in the office yet. So, I parked and waited. Finally, someone called the manager, and she was kind enough to come and show me where my apartment was and gave me the key. The electric was already on, so I turned on the air conditioner and took a shower and a nap. In the early afternoon, Jason, his girlfriend, and his step-brother arrived to move me in, up two flights of stairs. Then we had a late lunch when they finished. I went to my old Pub that night to say hello. There were a lot of the old crowd there. One of them is a song writer and wrote a hit for Bernie Higgins. I don't think he'd had any recent hits though. It was good to see him and everyone else and to have a pint of Guinness beer. Nothing like it!

I spent the next week filling out applications. Then I went to my cousin David Leigh's home to visit. I got a phone call while I was there that I had a job at a Psychiatric Hospital to start that coming Monday. I had to cut my visit short. I found out David had sold off his parents' home to people who wanted a butterfly farm. The place had lots of trees and bushes and a natural spring. My cousin had gotten rid of everything. Quilts, antiquities, and so on. I was a little angry that I got none of it. Oh, well, out of sight, out of mind, I guess. He had become ill with Interstitial Fibrosis and had months to live. Bless him, he gave me his slightly used Toyota.

I started work that Monday and lost my job after three months due to my tone of voice. Sorry, I explained I had grown up in a Marine Corps household. Everyone in my family tended to have a strong tone of voice. It helped in my work. I never had to call a "code" on my unit, and I believe that is why.

Once I got back to Florida, my home, I swear I'll never move away again. This is my story. New ones are beginning every day.

The Florida sun came up bright and hot as usual for a day in late August...